❧

SHAKESPEARE'S HISTORY

OF

KING HENRY V.

❧

King Henry
V.

SHAKESPEARE'S

HISTORY OF

KING HENRY THE FIFTH

EDITED, WITH NOTES,

BY

WILLIAM J. ROLFE, Litt. D.,

FORMERLY HEAD MASTER OF THE HIGH SCHOOL, CAMBRIDGE. MASS.

WITH ENGRAVINGS.

NEW YORK ∴ CINCINNATI ∴ CHICAGO

AMERICAN BOOK COMPANY

ENGLISH CLASSICS.

Edited by WM. J. ROLFE, Litt. D.

Illustrated. 12mo, Cloth, 56 cents per volume.

Shakespeare's Works.

The Merchant of Venice.	Richard III.
Othello.	Henry VIII.
Julius Cæsar.	King Lear
A Midsummer-Night's Dream.	The Taming of the Shrew.
Macbeth.	All 's Well that Ends Well.
Hamlet.	Coriolanus.
Much Ado about Nothing.	The Comedy of Errors.
Romeo and Juliet.	Cymbeline.
As You Like It.	Antony and Cleopatra.
The Tempest.	Measure for Measure.
Twelfth Night.	Merry Wives of Windsor.
The Winter's Tale.	Love's Labour 's Lost.
King John.	Two Gentlemen of Verona.
Richard II.	Timon of Athens.
Henry IV. Part I.	Troilus and Cressida.
Henry IV. Part II.	Pericles, Prince of Tyre.
Henry V.	The Two Noble Kinsmen.
Henry VI. Part I.	Venus and Adonis, Lucrece, etc.
Henry VI. Part II.	Sonnets.
Henry VI. Part III.	Titus Andronicus.

GOLDSMITH'S SELECT POEMS. BROWNING'S SELECT POEMS.
GRAY'S SELECT POEMS.   BROWNING'S SELECT DRAMAS.
MINOR POEMS OF JOHN MILTON. MACAULAY'S LAYS OF ANCIENT ROME.
    WORDSWORTH'S SELECT POEMS.

LAMBS' TALES FROM SHAKESPEARE'S COMEDIES.
LAMBS' TALES FROM SHAKESPEARE'S TRAGEDIES.
Edited by WM. J. ROLFE, Litt. D.
Illustrated. Cloth, 12mo, 50 cents per volume.

King Henry V.

W. P. 10

CONTENTS.

STREET IN HARFLEUR.

HENRY V.

INTRODUCTION

TO

KING HENRY THE FIFTH.

I. THE HISTORY OF THE PLAY.

King Henry the Fifth, in the form in which we now have it, was first published in the folio of 1623, where it occupies pages 69–95 in the division of "Histories." A mutilated and incomplete quarto edition had been printed in 1600 with the following title-page:

THE | CRONICLE | History of Henry the fift, | With his battell fought at *Agin Court* in | France. Togither with *Auntient* | *Pistoll.* | *As it hath bene sundry times playd by the Right honorable* | *the Lord Chamberlaine his seruants.* | LONDON | Printed by *Thomas Creede,* for Tho. Milling-|ton, and Iohn Busby. And are to be | sold at his house in Carter Lane, next | the Powle head. 1600.

This edition appears to have been hastily gotten up, and was probably compiled from short-hand notes taken at the theatre.

It was reprinted in 1602 "by Thomas Creede, for Thomas Pauier," and "sold at his shop in Cornhill, at the signe of the Cat and Parrets, neare the Exchange;" and again in 1608, "Printed for T. P."

The folio must be considered the only authority for the text, though the quartos are occasionally of service in the correction of typographical errors.

The date of the play is fixed by a passage in the Chorus of the last act:

"Were now the general of our gracious empress—
      As in good time he may—from Ireland coming," etc.

This evidently refers to Lord Essex, who went to Ireland, April 15, 1599, and returned to London, September 28, of the same year. Unless the passage was a later insertion, which is not probable, the play must have been written between those dates. It is not mentioned by Meres in 1598 in the list which includes *Richard II., Richard III., Henry IV.,* and *King John.**

II. THE HISTORICAL SOURCES OF THE PLAY.

Shakespeare took the leading incidents of his *Henry IV.* and *Henry V.* from an anonymous play entitled "The Famous Victories of Henry the Fifth," which was written at

* See the extract from Meres's *Palladis Tamia,* in our ed. of *A Midsummer-Night's Dream,* p. 9.

least as early as 1588,* and had a popularity far beyond its merits ; but he drew his historical materials mainly from Holinshed's " Chronicles of Englande, Scotlande, and Ireland," as the illustrative extracts from that author in our notes will show. As in the case of *Richard II.* (see our ed. of that play, p. 14), he doubtless used the second edition of Holinshed, published in 1586–87.

III. CRITICAL COMMENTS ON THE PLAY.

[*From Gervinus's " Shakespeare Commentaries."*†]

The whole interest of our play lies in the development of the ethical character of the hero. After the poet has delineated his careless youthful life in 1 *Henry IV.*, and in 2 *Henry IV.* has shown the sting of reflection and consideration piercing his soul as the period of self-dependence approaches, he now displays Henry as arrived at the post of his vocation, and exhibits the king acting up to his resolutions for the future. At the very beginning of the play we are at once informed of the utter change which has passed over him. The sinful nature is driven out of him by reflection, the current of reformation has suddenly scoured away the old faults ; as the wholesome strawberry ripens best " neighboured by fruit of baser quality," so his active practice, his intercourse with lower life and simple nature, has matured in him all those gifts which etiquette and court ceremony would never

---

* It was entered on the Registers of the Stationers' Company, May 14, 1594, to Thomas Creede, as " a booke intituled the Famous Victories of Henrye the Fyft, conteyninge the honorable battell of Agincourt," but it is known that the famous actor Tarlton, who died in 1588, took the part of the Clown in the play. The earliest printed edition that has come down to us bears date in 1598, and has the following title-page :

THE | FAMOUS VIC-|tories of Henry the | fifth : | Containing the Honou-|rable Battell of Agin-court : | *As it was plaide by the Queenes Maiesties* | *Players.* | LONDON | Printed by Thomas Creede, 1598.

† *Shakespeare Commentaries*, by Dr. G. G. Gervinus, translated by F. E. Bunnett : revised ed. (London, 1875), p. 340 fol. (by permission).

have produced in him, and which those now around him perceive in him with admiration. The poet expressly tells us, through the prelates who discuss the king in the first scene, that there are no miracles, either in his poetry or in the world, and that the natural grounds for this wonderful change are to be sought for really in the unpromising school of this apparently untutored man. There this many-sidedness was developed which now astonishes them in him, and on account of which he now appears equally acquainted with all things, ecclesiastical and secular, in the cabinet as in the field. He no longer squanders his now valuable time, but weighs it to the last grain; the curb of mildness and mercy is now placed on his passions, and even foreign lands conjecture that

> "his vanities forespent
> Were but the outside of the Roman Brutus,
> Covering discretion with a coat of folly." . . .

In his courtship and on the day of battle Henry is just as plain a king as if he had "sold his farm to buy his crown." He has shaken off his old dissolute companions, but the remembrances of that simple intercourse are recalled to our mind at every moment. The same inclination to rove about with the common man in his army, the old mildness and familiarity, and the same love for an innocent jest, exist in him now as then, without derogating in the least from his kingly dignity. He leaves his nobles waiting in his tent while he visits the posts of his soldiers; the old habit of night-watching is of use to him now; he sounds the disposition of individuals; he encourages them without high-sounding words; he fortifies them without ostentation; he can preach to them and solve moral scruples, and can make himself intelligible to them; he contrives a trick quite of the old kind in the moment of most gloomy suspense; like a brother, he borrows the cloak of the old Erpingham; he familiarly allows his countryman Fluellen to join freely in his conversation with the herald; and in his short appeal before the battle he declares all to be his brothers who on this Crispin's day shed their blood with him.

This contrast between his repose and calmness and his martial excitement, between his plain homely nature and the kingly heroic spirit which in the moment of action exercises dominion over him, is, however, not the only one in which the poet has exhibited him. The night before and the day during the battle, which form the centre of our play, is a period so prominent, and one in which such manifold moods, emotions, and passions, are roused and crossed, that the best opportunity was here afforded to the poet for exhibiting to our view this many-sided man in all the richness and the diversity of his nature. When the mind is quickened, he himself says, "the organs break up their drowsy grave, and newly move with casted slough and fresh legerity;" and thus is it with him in this great and decisive moment. We see him in a short time alternate between the most different emotions and positions, ever the same master over himself, or we may rather say, over the opportunity and the matter which lie for the moment before him. . . .

How popular after his old fashion, and at the same time how sublime, is his encouragement to the battle! How calm his last words to the French herald! How far is he from being over-hasty in giving credit to the victory! When he hears of the touching death of the noble York, how near is he to tears! and at the same moment, alarmed by a new tumult, how steeled to a bloody command! how impatiently furious at the last resistance! and at the moment when victory decides for him, how pious and how humble! And again, a short time after this solemn elevation of mind, he concludes his joke with Williams, careful even then that no harm should result from it. The poet has continued in the fifth act to show us to the very last the many-sided nature of the king. The terrible warrior is transformed into the merry bridegroom, the humorous vein again rises within him ; yet he is not so much in love with his happiness, or so happy in his love, that in the midst of his wooing, and with all his jest and repartee, he would relax the smallest article of the peace which his policy had designed. . . .

Throughout the whole play, throughout the whole bearing of the king, sounds the key-note of a religious composure, of a severe conscientiousness, and of a humble modesty. The Chronicle, which extols Henry so highly that it placed him before the poet as an historical favourite, praises the king's piety at home and at every page in his campaign; Shakespeare accepted this historical hint in no mechanical manner, but wrought it appropriately into the characteristics of his hero. The clergy, at the very beginning of the play, call him a true friend of the Church, and have reason to rejoice over his respect for it, as well as over his knowledge of sacred things. When he is occupied with the plan of war, he charges the Archbishop of Canterbury with a solemn oath to take heed in his counsel ; he " will believe in heart " that what he speaks as to his right to this war is in his " conscience washed as pure as sin with baptism." When he has no thought but France, those to God alone " run before " his business. He receives it as a promising ordinance from God that the treason lurking in his way is "brought to light." He delivers his " puissance into the hand of God, putting it straight in expedition ;" " God before," he says several times, he will come to take his right. He orders his old friend Bardolph to be pitilessly executed for robbing a church ; he wishes all such offenders to be cut off ; for he well knows that when " lenity and cruelty play for a kingdom, the gentler gamester is the soonest winner." We have seen him previous to the battle in solemn preparation, and engaged in edifying conversation with his soldiers. His first word on the certainty of the victory is, " Praised be God, and not our strength, for it !" When he reviews the greatness of the victory, he says

again, "Take it, God, for it is only thine!" And that this is
in earnest, he orders even death to be proclaimed to any who
may boast of it or take the honour from God. At his tri-
umphal entry into London, he forbids the sword and helm,
the trophies of his warlike deeds, to be borne before him ;
and the poet says expressly of him, in the prologue, what
once the prince had said of himself on that day at Shrews-
bury over Percy's body—that he was " free from vainness
and self-glorious pride, giving full trophy, signal, and ostent,
quite from himself to God." The atonement which his father
could not attain to, for want of energetic, persevering, inward
stimulus, is accomplished by him. In his prayer to God before the battle, when he wishes that " the sense of reckoning"
may be taken from his soldiers, and that his father's fault
may not be thought upon, he declares that he has "interred
anew" Richard's body, has wept over it, and has ordered
masses to be said ; that he has five hundred poor in yearly
pay "who twice a day their withered hands hold up toward
Heaven" for him. The poet, we see plainly, adheres to the
character of the age, and invests Henry with all that outward
work of repentance which in that day was considered necessary for the expiation of a crime. To many he will appear
to have gone too far in this, both as regards his hero, who is
otherwise of so unshackled a mind, and himself, rising as he
does generally so far above the narrow views of his own, to
say nothing of older times. But above this objection, also,
the poet soars victoriously in those excellent words which he
puts into the mouth of the king at the close of that peniten-
tial prayer :

> "More will I do ;
> Though all that I can do is little worth,
> Since that my penitence comes after all,
> Imploring pardon "

[*From Dowden's " Shakspere."* *]

Henry's freedom from egoism, his modesty, his integrity his joyous humour, his practical piety, his habit of judging things by natural and not artificial standards—all these are various developments of the central element of his character, his noble realization of fact.

But his realization of fact produces something more than this integrity, this homely honesty of nature. It breathes through him an enthusiasm which would be intense if it were not so massive. Through his union with the vital strength of the world, he becomes one of the world's most glorious and beneficent forces. From the plain and mirth-creating comrade of his fellow-soldiers he rises into the genius of impassioned battle. From the modest and quiet adviser with his counsellors and prelates, he is transformed, when the occasion requires it, into the terrible administrator of justice. When Henry takes from his father's pillow the crown, and places it upon his own head, the deed is done with no fluttering rapture of attainment. He has entered gravely upon his manhood. He has made very real to himself the long, careful, and joyless life of his father who had won for him this "golden care." His heart is full of tenderness for this sad father, to whom he had been able to bring so little happiness. But now he takes his due, the crown, and the world's whole force shall not wrest it from him :

> " Thy due from me
> Is tears, and heavy sorrows of the blood,
> Which nature, love, and filial tenderness
> Shall, O dear father, pay thee plenteously:
> My due from thee is this imperial crown,
> Which, as immediate from thy place and blood,
> Derives itself to me. Lo, here it sits,

* *Shakspere. a Critical Study of his Mind and Art*, by Edward Dowden (2d ed. London, 1876), p. 215 fol. (by permission).

Which God shall guard; and put the world's whole strength
Into one giant arm, it shall not **force**
This lineal honour from me."

Here is no æsthetic feeling for the "situation," only **the** profoundest and noblest entrance into the fact. . . .

Shortly before the English army sets sail for France, the treason of Cambridge, Sctoop, and Grey is disclosed to the king. He does not betray his acquaintance with their designs. Surrounded by traitors, he boldly enters his council-chamber at Southampton (the wind is sitting fair, and but one deed remains to do before they go aboard). On the preceding day a man was arrested who had railed against the person of the king. Henry gives orders that he be set at liberty :

"We consider
It was excess of wine that set him on;
And on his more advice we pardon him."

But Scroop and Grey and Cambridge interpose. It would be true mercy, they insist, to punish such an offender. And then, when they have unawares brought themselves within the range of justice, Henry unfolds their guilt. The wrath of Henry has in it some of that awfulness and terror suggested by the apocalyptic reference to "the wrath of the Lamb." It is the more terrible because it transcends all egoistic feeling. What fills the king with indignation is not so much that his life should have been conspired against by men on whom his bounty has been bestowed without measure, as that they should have revolted against the loyalty of man, weakened the bonds of fellowship, and lowered the high tradition of humanity :

"O, how hast thou with jealousy **infected**
The sweetness of affiance ! Show men **dutiful** ?
Why, so didst thou : seem they grave and learned ?
Why, so didst thou : come they of noble family ?
Why, so didst thou : seem they religious ?

B

> Why, so didst thou: or are they spare in diet,
> Free from gross passion or of mirth or anger,
> Constant in spirit, not swerving with the blood,
> Garnish'd and deck'd in modest complement,
> Not working with the eye without the ear,
> And but in purged judgment trusting neither?
> Such and so finely bolted didst thou seem:
> And thus thy fall hath left a kind of blot,
> To mark the full-fraught man and best indued
> With some suspicion. I will weep for thee:
> For this revolt of thine, methinks, is like
> Another fall of man."

No wonder that the terrible moral insistance of these words
can subdue consciences made of penetrable stuff; no wonder
that such an awful discovery of high realities of life should
call forth the loyalty that lurked within a traitor's heart. But
though tears escape Henry he cannot relent:

> "Touching our person seek we no revenge;
> But we our kingdom's safety must so tender,
> Whose ruin you have sought, that to her laws
> We do deliver you. Get you therefore hence,
> Poor miserable wretches, to your death;
> The taste whereof, God of his mercy give
> You patience to endure, and true repentance
> Of all your dear offences!"

And having vindicated the justice of God, and purged his
country of treason, Henry sets his face to France with the
light of splendid achievement in his eyes.

On the night before the great battle, Henry moves among
his soldiers, and passes disguised from sentinel to sentinel.
He is not, like his father, exhausted and outworn by the careful construction of a life. If an hour of depression comes
upon him, he yet is strong, because he can look through his
depression to a strength and virtue outside of and beyond
himself. Joy may ebb within him or rise, as it will; the current of his inmost being is fed by a source that springs from
the hard rock of life, and is no tidal flow. He accepts his

weakness and his weariness as part of the surrender of ease and strength and self which he makes on behalf of England. With a touch of his old love of frolic he enters on the quarrel with Williams, and exchanges gages with the soldier. When morning dawns he looks freshly, and "overbears attaint," with cheerful semblance and sweet majesty:

> "A largess universal like the sun
> His liberal eye doth give to every one,
> Thawing cold fear."

With a prayer to God he sets to rights the heavenward side of his nature, and there leaves it. In the battle Henry does not, in the manner of his politic father, send into the field a number of counterfeit kings to attract away from himself the centre of the war. There is no stratagem at Agincourt; it is "plain shock and even play of battle." If Henry for a moment ceases to be the skilful wielder of resolute strength, it is only when he rises into the genius of the rage of battle:

> "I was not angry since I came to France
> Until this instant.—Take a trumpet, herald;
> Ride thou unto the horsemen on yon hill:
> If they will fight with us, bid them come down,
> Or void the field; they do offend our sight.
> If they'll do neither, we will come to them,
> And make them skirr away as swift as stones
> Enforced from the old Assyrian slings.
> Besides, we'll cut the throats of those we have,
> And not a man of them that we shall take
> Shall taste our mercy."

It is in harmony with the spirit of the play, and with the character of Henry, that it should close with no ostentatious heroics, but with the half jocular, whole earnest wooing of the French princess by the English king.

King Henry. Give me any gage of thine (iv. 1. 196).

KING HENRY V.

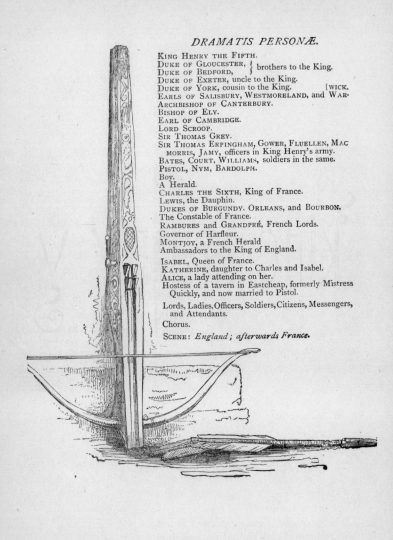

DRAMATIS PERSONÆ.

KING HENRY THE FIFTH.
DUKE OF GLOUCESTER, } brothers to the King.
DUKE OF BEDFORD,
DUKE OF EXETER, uncle to the King.
DUKE OF YORK, cousin to the King. [WICK.
EARLS OF SALISBURY, WESTMORELAND, and WAR-
ARCHBISHOP OF CANTERBURY.
BISHOP OF ELY.
EARL OF CAMBRIDGE.
LORD SCROOP.
SIR THOMAS GREY.
SIR THOMAS ERPINGHAM, GOWER, FLUELLEN, MAC
MORRIS, JAMY, officers in King Henry's army.
BATES, COURT, WILLIAMS, soldiers in the same.
PISTOL, NYM, BARDOLPH.
Boy.
A Herald.
CHARLES THE SIXTH, King of France.
LEWIS, the Dauphin.
DUKES OF BURGUNDY, ORLEANS, and BOURBON.
The Constable of France.
RAMBURES and GRANDPRÉ, French Lords.
Governor of Harfleur.
MONTJOY, a French Herald
Ambassadors to the King of England.

ISABEL, Queen of France.
KATHERINE, daughter to Charles and Isabel.
ALICE, a lady attending on her.
Hostess of a tavern in Eastcheap, formerly Mistress
Quickly, and now married to Pistol.

Lords, Ladies, Officers, Soldiers, Citizens, Messengers,
and Attendants.

Chorus.

SCENE: *England; afterwards France.*

THE PRESENCE-CHAMBER (SCENE II.)

PROLOGUE.

Enter Chorus.

Chorus. O for a Muse of fire, that would ascend
The brightest heaven of invention,
A kingdom for a stage, princes to act,
And monarchs to behold the swelling scene!

Then should the warlike Harry, like himself,
Assume the port of Mars; and at his heels,
Leash'd in like hounds, should famine, sword, and fire
Crouch for employment.   But pardon, gentles all,
The flat unraised spirit that hath dar'd
On this unworthy scaffold to bring forth   10
So great an object: can this cockpit hold
The vasty fields of France? or may we cram
Within this wooden O the very casques
That did affright the air at Agincourt?
O, pardon! since a crooked figure may
Attest in little place a million;
And let us, ciphers to this great accompt,
On your imaginary forces work.
Suppose within the girdle of these walls
Are now confin'd two mighty monarchies,   20
Whose high-upreared and abutting fronts
The perilous, narrow ocean parts asunder.
Piece out our imperfections with your thoughts;
Into a thousand parts divide one man,
And make imaginary puissance:
Think, when we talk of horses, that you see them
Printing their proud hoofs i' the receiving earth;
For 't is your thoughts that now must deck our kings,
Carry them here and there, jumping o'er times,
Turning the accomplishment of many years   30
Into an hour-glass: for the which supply,
Admit me Chorus to this history;
Who prologue-like your humble patience pray,
Gently to hear, kindly to judge, our play.   [*Exit.*

ACT I.

SCENE I. *London. An Ante-chamber in the King's Palace.*

Enter the ARCHBISHOP OF CANTERBURY *and the* BISHOP OF ELY.

Canterbury. My lord, I 'll tell you; that self bill is urg'd,
Which in the eleventh year of the last king's reign
Was like, and had indeed against us pass'd,
But that the scambling and unquiet time
Did push it out of farther question.
  Ely. But how, my lord, shall we resist it now?
  Canterbury. It must be thought on. If it pass against us,
We lose the better half of our possession;
For all the temporal lands which men devout
By testament have given to the church   10
Would they strip from us; being valued thus:
As much as would maintain, to the king's honour.
Full fifteen earls and fifteen hundred knights,
Six thousand and two hundred good esquires;
And, to relief of lazars and weak age,
Of indigent faint souls past corporal toil,
A hundred almshouses right well supplied;
And to the coffers of the king beside,
A thousand pounds by the year: thus runs the bill.
  Ely. This would drink deep.
  Canterbury.   'T would drink the cup and all.   20
  Ely. But what prevention?
  Canterbury. The king is full of grace and fair regard.
  Ely. And a true lover of the holy church.
  Canterbury. The courses of his youth promis'd it not.
The breath no sooner left his father's body,
But that his wildness, mortified in him,
Seem'd to die too; yea, at that very moment
Consideration, like an angel, came

And whipp'd the offending Adam out of him,
Leaving his body as a paradise   30
To envelope and contain celestial spirits.
Never was such a sudden scholar made;
Never came reformation in a flood
With such a heady currance, scouring faults;
Nor never hydra-headed wilfulness
So soon did lose his seat and all at once
As in this king.

  Ely.   We are blessed in the change.

  Canterbury. Hear him but reason in divinity,
And, all-admiring, with an inward wish
You would desire the king were made a prelate: 40
Hear him debate of commonwealth affairs,
You would say it hath been all in all his study:
List his discourse of war, and you shall hear
A fearful battle render'd you in music:
Turn him to any cause of policy,
The Gordian knot of it he will unloose,
Familiar as his garter: that, when he speaks,
The air, a charter'd libertine, is still,
And the mute wonder lurketh in men's ears,
To steal his sweet and honey'd sentences;   50
So that the art and practic part of life
Must be the mistress to this theoric:
Which is a wonder how his grace should glean it.
Since his addiction was to courses vain,
His companies unletter'd, rude, and shallow,
His hours fill'd up with riots, banquets, sports,
And never noted in him any study,
Any retirement, any sequestration
From open haunts and popularity.

  Ely. The strawberry grows underneath the nettle,   60
And wholesome berries thrive and ripen best
Neighbour'd by fruit of baser quality:

And so the prince obscur'd his contemplation
Under the veil of wildness; which, no doubt,
Grew like the summer grass, fastest by night,
Unseen, yet crescive in his faculty.

   Canterbury. It must be so; for miracles are ceas'd,
And therefore we must needs admit the means
How things are perfected.

   Ely.   But, my good lord,
How now for mitigation of this bill   70
Urg'd by the commons?   Doth his majesty
Incline to it, or no?

   Canterbury.   He seems indifferent,
Or rather swaying more upon our part
Than cherishing the exhibiters against us;
For I have made an offer to his majesty,—
Upon our spiritual convocation
And in regard of causes now in hand,
Which I have open'd to his grace at large,
As touching France,—to give a greater sum
Than ever at one time the clergy yet   80
Did to his predecessors part withal.

   Ely. How did this offer seem receiv'd, my lord?

   Canterbury. With good acceptance of his majesty;
Save that there was not time enough to hear,
As I perceiv'd his grace would fain have done,
The severals and unhidden passages
Of his true titles to some certain dukedoms,
And generally to the crown and seat of France
Deriv'd from Edward, his great-grandfather.

   Ely. What was the impediment that broke this off?   90

   Canterbury. The French ambassador upon that instant
Crav'd audience; and the hour, I think, is come
To give him hearing: is it four o'clock?

   Ely. It is.

   Canterbury.   Then go we in, to know his embassy;

Which I could with a ready guess declare,
Before the Frenchman speak a word of it.
    Ely. I 'll wait upon you, and I long to hear it.   [*Exeunt.*

SCENE II.   *The same.   The Presence-chamber.*

Enter KING HENRY, GLOUCESTER, BEDFORD, EXETER, WAR-
    WICK, WESTMORELAND, *and* Attendants.

    King Henry. Where is my gracious Lord of Canterbury?
    Exeter. Not here in presence.
    King Henry.   Send for him, good uncle.
    Westmoreland. Shall we call in the ambassador, my liege?
    King Henry. Not yet, my cousin: we would be resolv'd,
Before we hear him, of some things of weight
That task our thoughts, concerning us and France.

Enter the ARCHBISHOP OF CANTERBURY *and the* BISHOP
    OF ELY.

    Canterbury. God and his angels guard your sacred throne,
And make you long become it!
    King Henry.   Sure, we thank you.
My learned lord, we pray you to proceed
And justly and religiously unfold   10
Why the law Salique that they have in France
Or should, or should not, bar us in our claim.
And God forbid, my dear and faithful lord,
That you should fashion, wrest, or bow your reading,
Or nicely charge your understanding soul
With opening titles miscreate, whose right
Suits not in native colours with the truth:
For God doth know how many now in health
Shall drop their blood in approbation
Of what your reverence shall incite us to.   20
Therefore take heed how you impawn our person,
How you awake our sleeping sword of war:

We charge you, in the name of God, take **heed** ;
For never two such kingdoms did contend
Without much fall of blood; whose guiltless **drops**
Are every one a woe, a sore complaint
'Gainst him whose wrong gives edge unto the **swords**
That make such waste in brief mortality.
Under this conjuration speak, my lord;
For we will hear, note, and believe in heart   **30**
That what you speak is in your conscience wash'd
As pure as sin with baptism.
    Canterbury. Then hear me, gracious sovereign, and you
        peers,
That owe yourselves, your lives, and services
To this imperial throne.   There is no bar
To make against your highness' claim to France
But this, which they produce from Pharamond,—
' In terram Salicam mulieres ne succedant:'
' No woman shall succeed in Salique land;'
Which Salique land the French unjustly **gloze**   **40**
To be the realm of France, and Pharamond
The founder of this law and female bar.
Yet their own authors faithfully affirm
That the land Salique is in Germany,
Between the floods of Sala and of Elbe;
Where Charles the Great, having subdued the Saxons,
There left behind and settled certain French ;
Who, holding in disdain the German women
For some dishonest manners of their life,
Establish'd then this **law** ; to wit, no female   **50**
Should be inheritrix in Salique land:
Which Salique, as I said, 'twixt Elbe and **Sala,**
Is at this day in Germany call'd Meisen.
Then doth it well appear the Salique law
Was not devised for the realm of France :
Nor did the French possess the Salique land

Until four hundred one and twenty years
After defunction of King Pharamond,
Idly suppos'd the founder of this law,
Who died within the year of our redemption   60
Four hundred twenty-six; and Charles the Great
Subdued the Saxons, and did seat the French
Beyond the river Sala, in the year
Eight hundred five.   Besides, their writers say,
King Pepin, which deposed Childeric,
Did, as heir general, being descended
Of Blithild, which was daughter to King Clothair,
Make claim and title to the crown of France.
Hugh Capet also,—who usurp'd the crown
Of Charles the duke of Lorraine, sole heir male   70
Of the true line and stock of Charles the Great,—
To fine his title with some shows of truth,
Though, in pure truth, it was corrupt and naught,
Convey'd himself as heir to the Lady Lingare,
Daughter to Charlemain, who was the son
To Lewis the emperor, and Lewis the son
Of Charles the Great.   Also King Lewis the Tenth,
Who was sole heir to the usurper Capet,
Could not keep quiet in his conscience,
Wearing the crown of France, till satisfied   80
That fair Queen Isabel, his grandmother,
Was lineal of the Lady Ermengare,
Daughter to Charles the foresaid duke of Lorraine:
By the which marriage the line of Charles the Great
Was re-united to the crown of France.
So that, as clear as is the summer's sun,
King Pepin's title and Hugh Capet's claim,
King Lewis his satisfaction, all appear
To hold in right and title of the female.
So do the kings of France unto this day;   90
Howbeit they would hold up this Salique law

To bar your highness claiming from the female,
And rather choose to hide them in a net
Than amply to imbare their crooked titles
Usurp'd from you and your progenitors.

King Henry. May I with right and conscience make this
    claim?

Canterbury. The sin upon my head, dread sovereign!
For in the book of Numbers is it writ,
When the man dies, let the inheritance
Descend unto the daughter.   Gracious lord,   100
Stand for your own; unwind your bloody flag;
Look back into your mighty ancestors:
Go, my dread lord, to your great-grandsire's tomb,
From whom you claim; invoke his warlike spirit,
And your great-uncle's, Edward the Black Prince,
Who on the French ground play'd a tragedy,
Making defeat on the full power of France,
Whiles his most mighty father on a hill
Stood smiling to behold his lion's whelp
Forage in blood of French nobility.   110
O noble English, that could entertain
With half their forces the full pride of France,
And let another half stand laughing by,
All out of work and cold for action!

Ely. Awake remembrance of these valiant dead,
And with your puissant arm renew their feats.
You are their heir; you sit upon their throne;
The blood and courage that renowned them
Runs in your veins; and my thrice-puissant liege
Is in the very May-morn of his youth,   120
Ripe for exploits and mighty enterprises.

Exeter. Your brother kings and monarchs of the earth
Do all expect that you should rouse yourself,
As did the former lions of your blood.

Westmoreland. They know your grace hath cause and
    means and might;

So hath your highness; never king of England
Had nobles richer and more loyal subjects,
Whose hearts have left their bodies here in England
And lie pavilion'd in the fields of France.

    Canterbury. O, let their bodies follow, my dear liege,   130
With blood and sword and fire to win your right;
In aid whereof we of the spiritualty
Will raise your highness such a mighty sum
As never did the clergy at one time
Bring in to any of your ancestors.

    King Henry. We must not only arm to invade the French,
But lay down our proportions to defend
Against the Scot, who will make road upon us
With all advantages.

    Canterbury. They of those marches, gracious sovereign, 140
Shall be a wall sufficient to defend
Our inland from the pilfering borderers.

    King Henry. We do not mean the coursing snatchers only,
But fear the main intendment of the Scot,
Who hath been still a giddy neighbour to us;
For you shall read that my great-grandfather
Never went with his forces into France
But that the Scot on his unfurnish'd kingdom
Came pouring, like the tide into a breach,
With ample and brim fulness of his force, 150
Galling the gleaned land with hot assays,
Girding with grievous siege castles and towns;
That England, being empty of defence,
Hath shook and trembled at the ill neighbourhood.

    Canterbury. She hath been then more fear'd than harm'd,
      my liege;
For hear her but exampled by herself:
When all her chivalry hath been in France,
And she a mourning widow of her nobles,
She hath herself not only well defended,

But taken and impounded as a stray   160
The King of Scots; whom she did send to France,
To fill King Edward's fame with prisoner **kings,**
And make her chronicle as rich with praise
As is the ooze and bottom of the sea
With sunken wrack and sumless treasuries.

    Westmoreland. But there's a saying very old **and** true,
            'If that you will France win,
               Then with Scotland first begin:'
For **once the** eagle England being in prey,
To her unguarded nest the weasel Scot   170
Comes sneaking, and so sucks her princely eggs,
Playing the mouse in absence of the cat,
To tear **and** havoc more than she can eat.

    Exeter. **It** follows **then** the cat must stay **at ho**me:
Yet that is **but a** curst necessity,
Since we **have locks** to safeguard necessaries,
And pretty traps to catch the petty thieves.
While that the armed hand doth fight abroad,
The advised head defends itself at home;
For government, though high and low **and** lower,
Put into parts, doth keep in one consent,
Congreeing in a full **and natural close,**
Like music.

    Canterbury. **Therefore doth heaven divide**
The state of man in divers functions,
Setting endeavour in continual motion;
To which is fixed, as an aim or butt,
Obedience: for so work the honey-bees,
Creatures that by a rule in nature teach
The act of order to a peopled kingdom.
They have a king and officers of sorts;   190
Where some, like magistrates, correct at home,
Others, like merchants, venture trade abroad,
Others, like soldiers, armed in their stings,

C

Make boot upon the summer's velvet buds,
Which pillage they with merry march bring **home**
To the tent-royal of their emperor;
Who, busied in his majesty, surveys
The singing masons building roofs of **gold**,
The civil citizens kneading up the honey,
The poor mechanic porters crowding in   200
Their heavy burdens at his narrow gate,
The sad-eyed justice, with his surly hum,
Delivering o'er to executors pale
The lazy yawning drone.   I this infer,
That many things, having full reference
To one consent, may work contrariously:
As many arrows, loosed several ways,
Come to one mark, as many ways meet in one **town**,
As many fresh streams meet in one salt sea,
As many lines close in the dial's centre;   210
So may a thousand actions, once afoot,
End in one purpose, and be all well borne
Without defeat.   Therefore to France, my liege.
Divide your happy England into four;
Whereof take you one quarter into France,
And you withal shall make all Gallia shake.
If we, with thrice such powers left at home,
Cannot defend our own doors from the dog,
Let us be worried, and our nation lose
The name of hardiness and policy.   220

    King Henry. Call in the messengers sent from the Dauphin.
                          [Exeunt some Attendants.

Now are we well resolv'd; and, by God's help,
And yours, the noble sinews of our power,
France being ours, we 'll bend it to our awe,
Or break it all to pieces: or there we 'll sit,
Ruling in large and ample empery
O'er France and all her almost kingly dukedoms.

Or **lay these** bones in an unworthy **urn,**
Tombless, with no remembrance over **them:**
Either **our** history shall with full mouth   230
Speak freely of our acts, or else our grave,
Like Turkish mute, shall have a tongueless **mouth,**
Not worshipp'd with a waxen epitaph.

Enter Ambassadors *of France.*

Now are we well prepar'd to know the pleasure
Of our fair cousin Dauphin; for we hear
Your greeting is from him, not from the king.
    First Ambassador. May 't please your majesty to give us
        leave
Freely to render what we have in charge;
Or shall we sparingly show you far off
The Dauphin's meaning and our embassy?   240
    King Henry. We are no tyrant, but a Christian king,
Unto whose grace our passion is as subject
As are our wretches fetter'd in our prisons:
Therefore with frank and with uncurbed plainness
Tell us the Dauphin's mind.
    First Ambassador.   Thus then, in few.
Your highness, lately sending into France,
Did claim some certain dukedoms, in the right
Of your great predecessor, King Edward the **Third.**
In answer of which claim, the prince our master
Says that you savour too much of your youth,   250
And bids you be advis'd there 's nought in **France**
That can be with a nimble galliard won;
You cannot revel into dukedoms there.
He therefore sends you, meeter for your spirit,
This tun of treasure; and, in lieu of this,
Desires you let the dukedoms that you claim
Hear no more of you.   This the Dauphin speaks.
    King Henry. What treasure, uncle?

Exeter.   Tennis-balls, my liege.

King Henry. We **are glad** the Dauphin is so pleasant
    with us;
His present and your pains we thank you for.   260
When we have match'd our rackets to these balls,
We will, in France, by God's grace, play a set
Shall strike his father's crown into the hazard.
Tell him he hath made a match with such a wrangler
That all the courts of France will be disturb'd
With chases.   And we understand him well,
How he comes o'er us with our wilder days,
Not measuring what use we made of them.
We never valued this poor seat of England,
And therefore, living hence, did give ourself   270
To barbarous license; as 't is ever common
That men are merriest when they are from home.
But tell the Dauphin I will keep my state,
Be like a king, and show my sail of greatness
When I do rouse me in my throne of France:
For that I have laid by my majesty
And plodded like a man for working-days,
But I will rise there with so full a glory
That I will dazzle all the eyes of France,
Yea, strike the Dauphin blind to look on us.   280
And tell the pleasant prince this mock of his
Hath turn'd his balls to gun-stones; and his soul
Shall stand sore charged for the wasteful vengeance
That shall fly with them: for many a thousand widows
Shall this his mock mock out of their dear husbands,
Mock mothers from their sons, mock castles down;
And some are yet ungotten and unborn
That shall have cause to curse the Dauphin's scorn
But this lies all within the will of God,
To whom I do appeal; and in whose name   290
Tell you the Dauphin I am coming on,

To venge me as I may, and to put forth
My rightful hand in a well-hallow'd cause.
So get you hence in peace; and tell the Dauphin
His jest will savour but of shallow wit,
When thousands weep more than did laugh at it.—
Convey them with safe conduct.—Fare you well.

> [*Exeunt Ambassador.*

   Exeter. This was a merry message.
   King Henry. We hope to make the sender blush at it.
Therefore, my lords, omit no happy hour   300
That may give furtherance to our expedition;
For we have now no thought in us but France,
Save those to God, that run before our business.
Therefore let our proportions for these wars
Be soon collected, and all things thought upon
That may with reasonable swiftness add
More feathers to our wings; for, God before,
We 'll chide this Dauphin at his father's door.
Therefore let every man now task his thought,
That this fair action may on foot be brought.   310

> [*Exeunt. Flourish.*

ROOM IN THE FRENCH KING'S PALACE (SCENE IV.).

ACT II.

PROLOGUE.

Enter Chorus.

Chorus. Now all the youth of England are on **fire**,
And silken dalliance in the wardrobe lies:
Now thrive the armourers, and honour's thou**ght**

Reigns solely in the breast of every man.
They sell the pasture now to buy the horse,
Following the mirror of all Christian kings,
With winged heels, as English Mercuries;
For now sits Expectation in the air,
And hides a sword from hilts unto the point
With crowns imperial, crowns, and coronets, 10
Promis'd to Harry and his followers.
The French, advis'd by good intelligence
Of this most dreadful preparation,
Shake in their fear, and with pale policy
Seek to divert the English purposes.
O England! model to thy inward greatness,
Like little body with a mighty heart,
What mightst thou do, that honour would thee do,
Were all thy children kind and natural!
But see thy fault! France hath in thee found out 20
A nest of hollow bosoms, which he fills
With treacherous crowns; and three corrupted men,
One, Richard Earl of Cambridge, and the second,
Henry Lord Scroop of Masham, and the third,
Sir Thomas Grey, knight, of Northumberland,
Have, for the gilt of France,—O guilt indeed!—
Confirm'd conspiracy with fearful France;
And by their hands this grace of kings must die,
If hell and treason hold their promises,
Ere he take ship for France, and in Southampton. 30
Linger your patience on, and well digest
The abuse of distance; force a play.
The sum is paid; the traitors are agreed;
The king is set from London; and the scene
Is now transported, gentles, to Southampton;
There is the playhouse now, there must you sit.
And thence to France shall we convey you safe,
And bring you back, charming the narrow seas

To give you gentle pass; for, if we may,
We 'll not offend one stomach with our play. 40
But, till the king come forth, and not till then,
Unto Southampton do we shift our scene. [*Exit.*

SCENE I. *London. A Street.*

Enter Corporal NYM *and* Lieutenant BARDOLPH.

Bardolph. Well met, Corporal Nym.

Nym. Good morrow, Lieutenant Bardolph.

Bardolph. What, are Ancient Pistol and you friends yet?

Nym. For my part, I care not: I say little; but when time shall serve, there shall be smiles; but that shall be as it may. I dare not fight; but I will wink and hold out mine iron: it is a simple one; but what though? it will toast cheese, and it will endure cold as another man's sword will: and there 's an end.

Bardolph. I will bestow a breakfast to make you friends; and we 'll be all three sworn brothers to France: let it be so, good Corporal Nym. 12

Nym. Faith, I will live so long as I may, that's the certain of it; and when I cannot live any longer, I will do as I may: that is my rest, that is the rendezvous of it.

Bardolph. It is certain, corporal, that he is married to Nell Quickly: and certainly she did you wrong; for you were troth-plight to her.

Nym. I cannot tell; things must be as they may: men may sleep, and they may have their throats about them at that time; and some say knives have edges. It must be as it may: though patience be a tired mare, yet she will plod. There must be conclusions. Well, I cannot tell. 23

Enter PISTOL *and* Hostess.

Bardolph. Here comes Ancient Pistol and his wife: good corporal, be patient here. How now, mine host Pistol!

Pistol. Base tike, call'st thou me host?
Now, by this hand, I swear, I scorn the term;
Nor shall my Nell keep lodgers.   28

Hostess. No, by my troth, not long; for we cannot lodge
and board a dozen or fourteen gentlewomen that live hon-
estly by the prick of their needles, but it will be thought we
keep a bawdy house straight. [*Nym and Pistol draw.*] O
well a day, Lady, if he be not drawn now! we shall see wil-
ful adultery and murder committed.

Bardolph. Good lieutenant! good corporal! offer nothing
here.

Nym. Pish!

Pistol. Pish for thee, Iceland dog! thou prick-ear'd cur
of Iceland!

Hostess. Good Corporal Nym, show thy valour, and put
up your sword.   41

Nym. Will you shog off? I would have you solus.

Pistol. 'Solus,' egregious dog? O viper vile!
The 'solus' in thy most mervailous face;
The 'solus' in thy teeth, and in thy throat,
And in thy hateful lungs, yea, in thy maw, perdy,
And, which is worse, within thy nasty mouth!
I do retort the 'solus' in thy bowels;
For I can take, and Pistol's cock is up,
And flashing fire will follow.   50

Nym. I am not Barbason; you cannot conjure me. I have
an humour to knock you indifferently well. If you grow
foul with me, Pistol, I will scour you with my rapier, as I
may, in fair terms: if you would walk off, I would prick your
guts a little, in good terms, as I may: and that's the humour
of it.

Pistol. O braggart vile, and damned furious wight!
The grave doth gape, and doting death is near;
Therefore exhale.   59

Bardolph. Hear me, hear me what I say: he that strikes

the first stroke, I 'll run him up to the hilts, as I am a
soldier.   [*Draws.*

Pistol. An oath of mickle might ; and fury shall abate.
Give me thy fist, thy fore-foot to me give ;
Thy spirits are most tall.

Nym. I will cut thy throat, one time or other, in fair
terms ; that is the humour of it.

Pistol. ' Couple a gorge ! '
That is the word.   I thee defy again.
O hound of Crete, think'st thou my spouse to get ?   70
No ; to the spital go,
And from the powdering-tub of infamy
Fetch forth the lazar kite of Cressid's kind,
Doll Tearsheet she by name, and her espouse :
I have, and I will hold, the quondam Quickly
For the only she ; and—pauca, there 's enough.
Go to.

Enter the Boy.

Boy. Mine host Pistol, you must come to my master,
and you, hostess ; he is very sick, and would to bed.—
Good Bardolph, put thy face between his sheets, and do
the office of a warming-pan.   Faith, he 's very ill.   81

Bardolph. Away, you rogue !

Hostess. By my troth, he'll yield the crow a pudding one
of these days.   The king has killed his heart.   Good husband, come home presently.   [*Exeunt Hostess and Boy.*

Bardolph. Come, shall I make you two friends ? We
must to France together : why the devil should we keep
knives to cut one another's throats ?

Pistol. Let floods o'erswell, and fiends for food howl
on !   90

Nym. You 'll pay me the eight shillings I won of you
at betting ?

Pistol. Base is the slave that pays.

Nym. That now I will have : that 's the humour of it.

Pistol. As manhood shall compound : push home.

[*They draw.*

Bardolph. By this sword, he that makes the first thrust, I 'll kiil him ; by this sword, I will.

Pistol. Sword is an oath, and oaths must have their course.

Bardolph. Corporal Nym, an thou wilt be friends, be friends ; an thou wilt not, why, then, be enemies with me too.   Prithee, put up.   101

Nym. I shall have my eight shillings I won of you at betting ?

Pistol. A noble shalt thou have, and present pay ;
And liquor likewise will I give to thee,
And friendship shall combine, and brotherhood :
I 'll live by Nym, and Nym shall live by me.
Is not this just ? for I shall sutler be
Unto the camp, and profits will accrue.
Give me thy hand.   110

Nym. I shall have my noble ?

Pistol. In cash most justly paid.

Nym. Well, then, that 's the humour of 't.

Re-enter Hostess.

Hostess. As ever you came of women, come in quickly to Sir John.   Ah, poor heart ! he is so shaked of a burning quotidian tertian, that it is most lamentable to behold. Sweet men, come to him.

Nym. The king hath run bad humours on the knight ; that 's the even of it.

Pistol. Nym, thou hast spoke the right ;   120
His heart is fracted and corroborate.

Nym. The king is a good king ; but it must be as it may : he passes some humours and careers.

Pistol. Let us condole the knight ; for lambkins we will
    live.

SCENE II. *Southampton.* *A Council-chamber.*

Enter EXETER, BEDFORD, *and* WESTMORELAND.

Bedford. Fore God, his grace is bold, to trust these traitors.

Exeter. They shall be apprehended by and by.

Westmoreland. How smooth and even they do bear them
selves !
As if allegiance in their bosoms sat,
Crowned with faith and constant loyalty.

Bedford. The king hath note of all that they intend,
By interception which they dream not of.

Exeter. Nay, but the man that was his bedfellow,
Whom he hath dull'd and cloy'd with gracious favours,—
That he should, for a foreign purse, so sell   10
His sovereign's life to death and treachery !

Trumpets sound. *Enter* KING HENRY, SCROOP, CAMBRIDGE,
GREY, *and* Attendants.

King Henry. Now sits the wind fair, and we will aboard.
My Lord of Cambridge, and my kind Lord of Masham,
And you, my gentle knight, give me your thoughts :
Think you not that the powers we bear with us
Will cut their passage through the force of France,
Doing the execution and the act
For which we have in head assembled them ?

Scroop. No doubt, my liege, if each man do his best.

King Henry. I doubt not that ; since we are well persuaded
We carry not a heart with us from hence   21
That grows not in a fair consent with ours,
Nor leave not one behind that doth not wish
Success and conquest to attend on us.

Cambridge. Never was monarch better fear'd and lov'd
Than is your majesty : there 's not, I think, a subject

That sits in heart-grief and uneasiness
Under the sweet shade of your government.

   Grey. True: those that were your father's enemies
Have steep'd their galls in honey, and do serve you   3ᵢ
With hearts create of duty and of zeal.

   King Henry. We therefore have great cause of thankful-
       ness;
And shall forget the office of our hand,
Sooner than quittance of desert and merit
According to the weight and worthiness.

   Scroop. So service shall with steeled sinews toil,
And labour shall refresh itself with hope,
To do your grace incessant services.

   King Henry. We judge no less.—Uncle of Exeter,
Enlarge the man committed yesterday,   40
That rail'd against our person: we consider
It was excess of wine that set him on;
And on his more advice we pardon him.

   Scroop. That's mercy, but too much security:
Let him be punish'd, sovereign, lest example
Breed, by his sufferance, more of such a kind.

   King Henry. O, let us yet be merciful.

   Cambridge. So may your highness, and yet punish too.

   Grey. Sir,
You show great mercy, if you give him life,   50
After the taste of much correction.

   King Henry. Alas, your too much care and love of
      me
Are heavy orisons 'gainst this poor wretch!
If little faults, proceeding on distemper,
Shall not be wink'd at, how shall we stretch our eye
When capital crimes, chew'd, swallow'd, and digested,
Appear before us?—We'll yet enlarge that man,
Though Cambridge, Scroop, and Grey, in their dear care
And tender preservation of our person,

Would have him punish'd.—And now to our French causes:
Who are the late commissioners?   61
 Cambridge. I one, my lord:
Your highness bade me ask for it to-day.
 Scroop. So did you me, my liege.
 Grey. And I, my royal sovereign.
 King Henry. Then, Richard Earl of Cambridge, there is
    yours;—
There yours, Lord Scroop of Masham;—and, sir knight,
Grey of Northumberland, this same is yours:—
Read them; and know, I know your worthiness.
My lord of Westmoreland, and uncle Exeter,   70
We will aboard to-night.—Why, how now, gentlemen!
What see you in those papers that you lose
So much complexion?—Look ye, how they change!
Their cheeks are paper.—Why, what read you there,
That hath so cowarded and chas'd your blood
Out of appearance?
 Cambridge.   I do confess my fault;
And do submit me to your highness' mercy.
 Grey.   }
 Scroop. } To which we all appeal.
 King Henry. The mercy that was quick in us but late,
By your own counsel is suppress'd and kill'd: 80
You must not dare, for shame, to talk of mercy;
For your own reasons turn into your bosoms,
As dogs upon their masters, worrying you.—
See you, my princes and my noble peers,
These English monsters! My lord of Cambridge here,—
You know how apt our love was to accord
To furnish him with all appertinents
Belonging to his honour; and this man
Hath, for a few light crowns, lightly conspir'd,
And sworn unto the practices of France,   90
To kill us here in Hampton: to the which

This knight, no less for bounty bound to us
Than Cambridge is, hath likewise sworn.—But, **O**,
What shall I say to thee, Lord Scroop? thou **cruel**,
Ingrateful, savage, and inhuman creature!
Thou that didst bear the key of all my counsels,
That knew'st the very bottom of my soul,
That almost mightst have coin'd me into gold,
Wouldst thou have practis'd on me for thy **use**,
May it be possible that foreign hire   100
Could out of thee extract one spark of evil
That might annoy my finger? 't is so strange,
That, though the truth of it stands off as gross
As black and white, my eye will scarcely see **it**.
Treason and murther ever kept together,
As two yoke-devils sworn to either's **purpose**,
Working so grossly in a natural cause,
That admiration did not whoop at them;
But thou, 'gainst all proportion, didst bring **in**
Wonder to wait on treason and on **murther**:   110
And whatsoever cunning fiend it was
That wrought upon thee so preposterously
Hath got the voice in hell for excellence.
All other devils that suggest by treasons
Do botch and bungle up damnation
With patches, colours, and with forms, being **fetch'd**
From glistering semblances of piety;
But he that temper'd thee bade thee stand up,
Gave thee no instance why thou should'st do **treason**,
Unless to dub thee with the name of traitor.   120
If that same demon that hath gull'd thee thus
Should with his lion gait walk the whole world,
He might return to vasty Tartar back,
And tell the legions, 'I can never win
A soul so easy as that Englishman's.'
O, how hast thou with jealousy infected

The sweetness of affiance!   Show men dutiful!
Why, so didst thou: seem they grave and learned?
Why, so didst thou: come they of noble family?
Why, so didst thou: seem they religious?   130
Why, so didst thou: or are they spare in diet,
Free from gross passion or of mirth or anger,
Constant in spirit, not swerving with the blood,
Garnish'd and deck'd in modest complement,
Not working with the eye without the ear,
And but in purged judgment trusting neither?
Such and so finely bolted didst thou seem:
And thus thy fall hath left a kind of blot,
To mark the full-fraught man and best indued
With some suspicion.   I will weep for thee;   140
For this revolt of thine, methinks, is like
Another fall of man.—Their faults are open:
Arrest them to the answer of the law;
And God acquit them of their practices!

  Exeter. I arrest thee of high treason, by the name
of Richard Earl of Cambridge.

  I arrest thee of high treason, by the name of Henry Lord
Scroop of Masham.

  I arrest thee of high treason, by the name of Thomas Grey,
knight, of Northumberland.   150

  Scroop. Our purposes God justly hath discover'd,
And I repent my fault more than my death;
Which I beseech your highness to forgive,
Although my body pay the price of it.

  Cambridge. For me, the gold of France did not seduce,
Although I did admit it as a motive
The sooner to effect what I intended:
But God be thanked for prevention;
Which I in sufferance heartily will rejoice,
Beseeching God and you to pardon me.   160

  Grey. Never did faithful subject more rejoice

At the discovery of most dangerous treason
Than I do at this hour joy o'er myself,
Prevented from a damned enterprise :
My fault, but not my body, pardon, sovereign.

    King Henry. God quit you in his mercy! Hear your sen
       tence.
You have conspir'd against our royal person,
Join'd with an enemy proclaim'd, and from his coffers
Receiv'd the golden earnest of our death ;
Wherein you would have sold your king to slaughter,   170
His princes and his peers to servitude,
His subjects to oppression and contempt,
And his whole kingdom into desolation.
Touching our person seek we no revenge ;
But we our kingdom's safety must so tender,
Whose ruin you have sought, that to her laws
We do deliver you.   Get you therefore hence,
Poor miserable wretches, to your death ;
The taste whereof, God of his mercy give
You patience to endure, and true repentance   180
Of all your dear offences !—Bear them hence.

       [Exeunt Cambridge, Scroop, and Grey, guarded.
Now, lords, for France ; the enterprise whereof
Shall be to you, as us, like glorious.
We doubt not of a fair and lucky war,
Since God so graciously hath brought to light
This dangerous treason lurking in our way
To hinder our beginnings. We doubt not now
But every rub is smoothed on our way.
Then forth, dear countrymen : let us deliver
Our puissance into the hand of God,   190
Putting it straight in expedition.
Cheerly to sea ; the signs of war advance :
No king of England, if not king of France.   *[Exeunt.*

          D

Scene III.   *London.   Before a Tavern.*

Enter Pistol, Hostess, Nym, Bardolph, *and* Boy.

Hostess. Prithee, honey-sweet husband, let me bring thee to Staines.

Pistol. No; for my manly heart doth yearn.—
Bardolph, be blithe: Nym, rouse thy vaunting veins:
Boy, bristle thy courage up; for Falstaff he is dead,
And we must yearn therefore.

Bardolph. Would I were with him, wheresome'er he is, either in heaven or in hell!

Hostess. Nay, sure, he's not in hell: he's in Arthur's bosom, if ever man went to Arthur's bosom. A' made a finer end, and went away an it had been any christom child; a' parted even just between twelve and one, even at the turning o' the tide: for after I saw him fumble with the sheets and play with flowers and smile upon his fingers' ends, I knew there was but one way; for his nose was as sharp as a pen, and a' babbled of green fields. 'How now, Sir John!' quoth I: 'what, man! be o' good cheer.' So a' cried out 'God, God, God!' three or four times. Now I, to comfort him, bid him a' should not think of God; I hoped there was no need to trouble himself with any such thoughts yet. So a' bade me lay more clothes on his feet: I put my hand into the bed and felt them, and they were as cold as any stone; then I felt to his knees, and they were as cold as any stone, and so upward and upward, and all was as cold as any stone.   24

Nym. They say he cried out of sack.

Hostess. Ay, that a' did.

Bardolph. And of women.

Hostess. Nay, that a' did not.

Boy. Yes, that a' did; and said they were devils incarnate.

Hostess. A' could never abide carnation; 't was a colour he never liked.   31

Boy. Do you not remember, a' saw a flea stick upon Bardolph's nose, and a' said it was a black soul burning in hell-fire?

Bardolph. Well, the fuel is gone that maintained that fire: that's all the riches I got in his service.

Nym. Shall we shog? the king will be gone from Southampton.

Pistol. Come, let's away.—My love, give me thy lips.
Look to my chattels and my movables: 40
Let senses rule; the word is 'Pitch and Pay:'
Trust none;
For oaths are straws, men's faiths are wafer-cakes,
And hold-fast is the only dog, my duck:
Therefore, Caveto be thy counsellor.
Go, clear thy crystals.—Yoke-fellows in arms,
Let us to France; like horse-leeches, my boys,
To suck, to suck, the very blood to suck!

Boy. And that's but unwholesome food, they say.

Pistol. Touch her soft mouth, and march.   50

Bardolph. Farewell, hostess.   [*Kissing her.*

Nym. I cannot kiss, that is the humour of it; but, adieu.

Pistol. Let housewifery appear: keep close, I thee command.

Hostess. Farewell; adieu.   [*Exeunt.*

SCENE IV. *France. A Room in the King's Palace.*

Flourish. Enter the FRENCH KING, *the* DAUPHIN, *the* DUKES
OF BERRI *and* BRETAGNE, *the* CONSTABLE, *and others.*

French King. Thus comes the English with full power
            upon us;
And more than carefully it us concerns
To answer royally in our defences.
Therefore the Dukes of Berri and of Bretagne,
Of Brabant and of Orleans, shall make forth,

And you, Prince Dauphin, with all swift dispatch,
To line and new repair our towns of war
With men of courage and with means defendant;
For England his approaches makes as fierce
As waters to the sucking of a gulf.
It fits us then to be as provident
As fear may teach us out of late examples
Left by the fatal and neglected English
Upon our fields.

    Dauphin.   My most redoubted father,
It is most meet we arm us 'gainst the foe;
For peace itself should not so dull a kingdom,
Though war nor no known quarrel were in question,
But that defences, musters, preparations,
Should be maintain'd, assembled, and collected,
As were a war in expectation.
Therefore, I say 't is meet we all go forth
To view the sick and feeble parts of France:
And let us do it with no show of fear;
No, with no more than if we heard that England
Were busied with a Whitsun morris-dance:
For, my good liege, she is so idly king'd,
Her sceptre so fantastically borne
By a vain, giddy, shallow, humorous youth,
That fear attends her not.

    Constable.   O peace, Prince Dauphin!
You are too much mistaken in this king:
Question your grace the late ambassadors,
With what great state he heard their embassy,
How well supplied with noble counsellors,
How modest in exception, and withal
How terrible in constant resolution,
And you shall find his vanities forespent
Were but the outside of the Roman Brutus,
Covering discretion with a coat of folly;

As gardeners do with ordure hide those roots
That shall first spring and be most delicate.   40
   Dauphin. Well, 't is not so, my lord high constable ;
But though we think it so, it is no matter :
In cases of defence 't is best to weigh
The enemy more mighty than he seems :
So the proportions of defence are fill'd ;
Which of a weak and niggardly projection
Doth, like a miser, spoil his coat with scanting
A little cloth.
   French King. Think we King Harry strong ;
And, princes, look you strongly arm to meet him.
The kindred of him hath been flesh'd upon us ;   50
And he is bred out of that bloody strain
That haunted us in our familiar paths.
Witness our too much memorable shame
When Cressy battle fatally was struck,
And all our princes captiv'd by the hand
Of that black name, Edward, Black Prince of Wales ;
Whiles that his mountain sire, on mountain standing,
Up in the air, crown'd with the golden sun,
Saw his heroical seed, and smil'd to see him,
Mangle the work of nature and deface   60
The patterns that by God and by French fathers
Had twenty years been made.   This is a stem
Of that victorious stock ; and let us fear
The native mightiness and fate of him.

Enter a Messenger.

   Messenger. Ambassadors from Harry King of England
Do crave admittance to your majesty.
   French King. We 'll give them present audience.   Go, and
      bring them.   [*Exeunt Messenger and certain Lords.*
You see this chase is hotly follow'd, friends.
   Dauphin. Turn head, and stop pursuit ; for coward dogs

Most spend their mouths when what they seem to threaten
Runs far before them.   Good my sovereign,   70
Take up the English short, and let them know
Of what a monarchy you are the head:
Self-love, my liege, is not so vile a sin
As self-neglecting.

Re-enter Lords, *with* EXETER *and train.*

French King.   From our brother England?
Exeter. From him; and thus he greets your majesty.
He wills you, in the name of God Almighty,
That you divest yourself, and lay apart
The borrow'd glories that by gift of heaven,
By law of nature and of nations, longs   80
To him and to his heirs; namely, the crown
And all wide-stretched honours that pertain
By custom and the ordinance of times
Unto the crown of France.   That you may know
'T is no sinister nor no awkward claim,
Pick'd from the worm-holes of long-vanish'd days,
Nor from the dust of old oblivion rak'd,
He sends you this most memorable line,
In every branch truly demonstrative,
Willing you overlook this pedigree;   90
And when you find him evenly deriv'd
From his most fam'd of famous ancestors,
Edward the Third, he bids you then resign
Your crown and kingdom, indirectly held
From him the native and true challenger.
French King. Or else what follows?
Exeter. Bloody constraint; for if you hide the crown
Even in your hearts, there will he rake for it:
Therefore in fiery tempest is he coming,
In thunder and in earthquake, like a Jove,   100
That, if requiring fail, he will compel;

And bids you, in the bowels of the Lord,
Deliver up the crown, and to take mercy
On the poor souls for whom this hungry war
Opens his vasty jaws; and on your head
Turning the widows' tears, the orphans' cries,
The dead men's blood, the pining maidens' groans,
For husbands, fathers, and betrothed lovers,
That shall be swallow'd in this controversy.
This is his claim, his threatening, and my message;   110
Unless the Dauphin be in presence here,
To whom expressly I bring greeting too.
   French King. For us, we will consider of this further:
To-morrow shall you bear our full intent
Back to our brother England.
   Dauphin.   For the Dauphin,
I stand here for him: what to him from England?
   Exeter. Scorn and defiance; slight regard, contempt,
And any thing that may not misbecome
The mighty sender, doth he prize you at.
Thus says my king; and if your father's highness   120
Do not, in grant of all demands at large,
Sweeten the bitter mock you sent his majesty,
He 'll call you to so hot an answer of it,
That caves and womby vaultages of France
Shall chide your trespass, and return your mock
In second accent of his ordinance.
   Dauphin. Say, if my father render fair return,
It is against my will; for I desire
Nothing but odds with England: to that end,
As matching to his youth and vanity,   130
I did present him with the Paris balls.
   Exeter. He 'll make your Paris Louvre shake for it,
Were it the mistress court of mighty Europe:
And, be assur'd, you 'll find a difference,
As we his subjects have in wonder found,

Between the promise of his greener days
And these he masters now.   Now he weighs time
Even to the utmost grain; that you shall read
In your own losses, if he stay in France.

    French King. To-morrow shall you know our mind at full.

    Exeter. Dispatch us with all speed, lest that our king   141
Come here himself to question our delay;
For he is footed in this land already.

    French King. You shall be soon dispatch'd with fair con-
        ditions:
A night is but small breath and little pause
To answer matters of this consequence.

                            [*Flourish.* [*Exeunt.*

ROUEN.

ACT III.

PROLOGUE.

Enter Chorus.

Chorus. Thus with imagin'd wing our swift scene flies,
In motion of no less celerity
Than that of thought. Suppose that you have seen
The well-appointed king at Hampton pier
Embark his royalty; and his brave fleet

With silken streamers the young Phœbus fanning:
Play with your fancies, and in them behold
Upon the hempen tackle ship-boys climbing;
Hear the shrill whistle which doth order give
To sounds confus'd; behold the threaden sails,   10
Borne with the invisible and creeping wind,
Draw the huge bottoms through the furrow'd sea,
Breasting the lofty surge.   O, do but think
You stand upon the rivage and behold
A city on the inconstant billows dancing;
For so appears this fleet majestical,
Holding due course to Harfleur.   Follow, follow!
Grapple your minds to sternage of this navy,
And leave your England, as dead midnight still,
Guarded with grandsires, babies, and old women,   20
Either past or not arriv'd to pith and puissance;
For who is he, whose chin is but enrich'd
With one appearing hair, that will not follow
These cull'd and choice-drawn cavaliers to France?
Work, work your thoughts, and therein see a siege;
Behold the ordnance on their carriages,
With fatal mouths gaping on girded Harfleur.
Suppose the ambassador from the French comes back;
Tells Harry that the king doth offer him
Katherine his daughter, and with her, to dowry,   30
Some petty and unprofitable dukedoms.
The offer likes not: and the nimble gunner
With linstock now the devilish cannon touches.

      [Alarum, and chambers go off.

And down goes all before them.   Still be kind,
And eke out our performance with your mind. *[Exit.*

SCENE I. *France. Before Harfleur.*

Alarum. Enter KING HENRY, EXETER, BEDFORD, GLOUCES
TER, *and* Soldiers, *with scaling-ladders.*

King Henry. Once more unto the breach, dear friends,
    once more,
Or close the wall up with our English dead!
In peace there 's nothing so becomes a man
As modest stillness and humility;
But when the blast of war blows in our ears,
Then imitate the action of the tiger:
Stiffen the sinews, summon up the blood,
Disguise fair nature with hard-favour'd rage,
Then lend the eye a terrible aspect;
Let it pry through the portage of the head   10
Like the brass cannon; let the brow o'erwhelm it
As fearfully as doth a galled rock
O'erhang and jutty his confounded base,
Swill'd with the wild and wasteful ocean.
Now set the teeth and stretch the nostril wide,
Hold hard the breath, and bend up every spirit
To his full height.   On, on, you noble English,
Whose blood is fet from fathers of war-proof,
Fathers that, like so many Alexanders,
Have in these parts from morn till even fought   20
And sheath'd their swords for lack of argument!
Dishonour not your mothers; now attest
That those whom you call'd fathers did beget you.
Be copy now to men of grosser blood,
And teach them how to war!—And you, good yeomen,
Whose limbs were made in England, show us here
The mettle of your pasture: let us swear
That you are worth your breeding; which I doubt not
For there is none of you so mean and base,

That hath not noble lustre in your eyes.   30
I see you stand like greyhounds in the slips,
Straining upon the start.   The game 's afoot:
Follow your spirit, and upon this charge
Cry 'God for Harry, England, and Saint George!'

> [*Exeunt.   Alarum, and chambers go off.*

SCENE II.   *The Same.   Another **Part of the Field.***

Enter NYM, BARDOLPH, PISTOL, *and* BOY.

Bardolph. On, on, on, on, on! to the breach, to the breach!

Nym. Pray thee, corporal, stay: the knocks are too hot;
and, for mine own part, I have not a case of lives: the humour of it is too hot, that is the very plain-song of it.

Pistol. The plain-song is most just, for humours do abound:
'Knocks go and come, God's vassals drop and die;

> And sword and shield,
> In bloody field,
> Doth win immortal fame.'

Boy. Would I were in an alehouse in London! I would
give all my fame for a pot of ale and safety.   11

Pistol. And I:

> 'If wishes would prevail with me,
> My purpose should not fail with me,
> But thither would I hie.'

Boy.   'As duly, but not as truly,
> As bird doth sing on bough.'

Enter FLUELLEN.

Fluellen. Up to the preach, you dogs! avaunt, you cullions!

> [*Driving them forward.*

Pistol. Be merciful, great duke, to men of mould!
Abate thy rage, abate thy manly rage,
Abate thy rage, great duke!   20
Good bawcock, bate thy rage; use lenity, sweet chuck!

Nym. These be good humours! your honour wins bad humours.   *[Exeunt all but Boy.*

Boy. As young as I am, I have observed these three swash-ers. I am boy to them all three: but all they three, though they would serve me, could not be man to me; for indeed three such antics do not amount to a man. For Bardolph. he is white-livered and red-faced; by the means whereof a' faces it out, but fights not. For Pistol, he hath a killing tongue and a quiet sword; by the means whereof a' breaks words, and keeps whole weapons. For Nym, he hath heard that men of few words are the best men; and therefore he scorns to say his prayers, lest a' should be thought a cow-ard: but his few bad words are matched with as few good deeds; for a' never broke any man's head but his own, and that was against a post when he was drunk. They will steal any thing, and call it purchase. Bardolph stole a lute-case, bore it twelve leagues, and sold it for three half-pence. Nym and Bardolph are sworn brothers in filching, and in Calais they stole a fire-shovel: I knew by that piece of service the men would carry coals. They would have me as familiar with men's pockets as their gloves or their handkerchers: which makes much against my manhood, if I should take from another's pocket to put into mine; for it is plain pock-eting up of wrongs. I must leave them, and seek some bet-ter service: their villany goes against my weak stomach, and therefore I must cast it up.   *[Exit.*

Enter FLUELLEN, GOWER *following.*

Gower. Captain Fluellen, you must come presently to the mines; the Duke of Gloucester would speak with you.   50

Fluellen. To the mines! tell you the duke, it is **not so** goot to come to the mines; for, look you, the mines is not accord-ing to the disciplines of the war: the concavities of it is not sufficient; for, look you, th' athversary. you may discuss unto the duke, look you, is digt himself four yard under the countermines. by Cheshu, I think a' will plow up all, if there is not petter directions.

Gower. The Duke of Gloucester, to whom the order of the siege is given, is altogether directed by an Irishman, a very valiant gentleman, i' faith.   60

Fluellen. It is Captain Macmorris, is it not?

Gower. I think it be.

Fluellen. By Cheshu, he is an ass, as in the world: I will verify as much in his peard: he has no more directions in the true disciplines of the wars, look you, of the Roman disciplines, than is a puppy-dog.

Enter MACMORRIS *and* Captain JAMY.

Gower. Here a' comes; and the Scots captain, Captain Jamy, with him.

Fluellen. Captain Jamy is a marvellous falorous gentleman, that is certain; and of great expedition and knowledge in th' aunchient wars, upon my particular knowledge of his directions: by Cheshu, he will maintain his argument as well as any military man in the world, in the disciplines of the pristine wars of the Romans.

Jamy. I say gud-day, Captain Fluellen.   75

Fluellen. God-den to your worship, goot Captain James.

Gower. How now, Captain Macmorris! have you quit the mines? have the pioners given o'er?

Macmorris. By Chrish, la! tish ill done: the work ish give over, the trumpet sound the retreat. By my hand, I swear, and my father's soul, the work ish ill done; it ish give over: I would have blowed up the town, so Chrish save me, la! in an hour. O, tish ill done, tish ill done; by my hand, tish ill done!

Fluellen. Captain Macmorris, I peseech you now, will you voutsafe me, look you, a few disputations with you, as partly touching or concerning the disciplines of the war, the Roman wars, in the way of argument, look you, and friendly commu-

nication, partly to satisfy my opinion, and partly for the satisfaction, look you, of my mind, as touching the direction of
the military discipline; that is the point.   91

Jamy. It sall be vary gud, gud feith, gud captains bath:
and I sall quit you with gud leve, as I may pick occasion;
that sall I, marry.

Macmorris. It is no time to discourse, so Chrish save me:
the day is hot, and the weather, and the wars, and the king,
and the dukes: it is no time to discourse. The town is be-
seeched, and the trumpet call us to the breach; and we talk,
and, be Chrish, do nothing: 't is shame for us all: so God sa'
me, 't is shame to stand still; it is shame, by my hand: and
there is throats to be cut, and works to be done; and there
ish nothing done, so Chrish sa' me, la!   102

Jamy. By the mess, ere these eyes of mine take themselves
to slomber, ay 'll do gud service, or ay 'll lig i' the grund for
it; ay, or go to death; and ay 'll pay 't as valorously as I may,
that sall I surely do, that is the breff and the long. Marry,
I wad full fain hear some question 'tween you tway.

Fluellen. Captain Macmorris, I think, look you, under your
correction, there is not many of your nation—

Macmorris. Of my nation! What ish my nation? What
ish my nation? Who talks of my nation ish a villain, and a
bastard, and a knave, and a rascal.   112

Fluellen. Look you, if you take the matter otherwise than
is meant, Captain Macmorris, peradventure I shall think you
do not use me with that affability as in discretion you ought
to use me, look you; peing as goot a man as yourself, poth
in the disciplines of war, and in the derivation of my pirth,
and in other particularities.

Macmorris. I do not know you so good a man as myself:
so Chrish save me, I will cut off your head.   120

Gower. Gentlemen both, you will mistake each other.

Jamy. Au! that 's a foul fault.   [*A parley sounded.*

Gower. The town sounds a parley.

Fluellen. Captain Macmorris, when there is more petter opportunity to pe required, look you, I will pe so pold as to tell you I know the disciplines of war; and there is an end.

[*Exeunt.*

SCENE III. *The Same. Before the Gates.*

The Governor *and some* Citizens *on the walls; the English forces below. Enter* KING HENRY *and his train.*

King Henry. How yet resolves the governor of the town?
This is the latest parle we will admit:
Therefore to our best mercy give yourselves;
Or, like to men proud of destruction,
Defy us to our worst; for, as I am a soldier,
A name that in my thoughts becomes me best,
If I begin the battery once again,
I will not leave the half-achieved Harfleur
Till in her ashes she lie buried.
The gates of mercy shall be all shut up,   10
And the flesh'd soldier, rough and hard of heart,
In liberty of bloody hand shall range
With conscience wide as hell, mowing like grass
Your fresh-fair virgins and your flowering infants.
What is it then to me, if impious war,
Array'd in flames, like to the prince of fiends,
Do, with his smirch'd complexion, all fell feats
Enlink'd to waste and desolation?
What is 't to me, when you yourselves are cause,
If your pure maidens fall into the hand   20
Of hot and forcing violation?
What rein can hold licentious wickedness
When down the hill he holds his fierce career?
We may as bootless spend our vain command
Upon the enraged soldiers in their spoil,
As send precepts to the leviathan

To come ashore.   Therefore, you men of Harfleur,
Take pity of your town and of your people,
Whiles yet my soldiers are in my command ;
Whiles yet the cool and temperate wind of grace
O'erblows the filthy and contagious clouds
Of heady murther, spoil, and villany.
If not, why, in a moment look to see
The blind and bloody soldier with foul hand
Defile the locks of your shrill-shrieking daughters ;
Your fathers taken by the silver beards.
And their most reverend heads dash'd to the walls ;
Your naked infants spitted upon pikes,
Whiles the mad mothers with their howls confus'd
Do break the clouds, as did the wives of Jewry
At Herod's bloody-hunting slaughtermen.
What say you? will you yield, and this avoid,
Or, guilty in defence, be thus destroy'd?

   Governor. Our expectation hath this day an end:
The Dauphin, whom of succours we entreated,
Returns us that his powers are yet not ready
To raise so great a siege.   Therefore, great king,
We yield our town and lives to thy soft mercy.
Enter our gates ; dispose of us and ours,
For we no longer are defensible.

   King Henry. Open your gates.—Come, uncle Exeter,
Go you and enter Harfleur ; there remain,
And fortify it strongly 'gainst the French :
Use mercy to them all.   For us, dear uncle,
The winter coming on, and sickness growing
Upon our soldiers, we will retire to Calais.
To-night in Harfleur will we be your guest ;
To-morrow for the march are we addrest.

      [*Flourish. The King and his train enter the town*
        E

Scene IV. *Rouen.   A Room in the Palace.*
Enter Katherine *and* Alice.

Katherine. Alice, tu as été en Angleterre, et tu parles bien
le langage.

Alice. Un peu, madame.

Katherine. Je te prie, m'enseignez ; il faut que j'apprenne
à parler.   Comment appelez-vous la main en Anglais?

Alice. La main? elle est appelée de hand.

Katherine. De hand.   Et les doigts?

Alice. Les doigts? ma foi, j'oublie les doigts? mais je me
souviendrai.   Les doigts? je pense qu'ils sont appelés de
fingres; oui, de fingres.   10

Katherine. La main, de hand; les doigts, de fingres.   Je
pense que je suis le bon écolier ; j'ai gagné deux mots
d'Anglais vîtement.   Comment appelez-vous les ongles?

Alice. Les ongles? nous les appelons de nails.

Katherine. De nails.   Écoutez; dites-moi, si je parle bien :
de hand, de fingres, et de nails.

Alice. C'est bien dit, madame ; il est fort bon Anglais.

Katherine. Dites-moi l'Anglais pour le bras.

Alice. De arm, madame.

Katherine. Et le coude?   20

Alice. De elbow.

Katherine. De elbow.   Je m'en fais la répétition de tous
les mots que vous m'avez appris dès à présent.

Alice. Il est trop difficile, madame, comme je pense.

Katherine. Excusez-moi, Alice ; écoutez: de hand, de fingres, de nails, de arm, de bilbow.

Alice. De elbow, madame.

Katherine. O Seigneur Dieu, je m'en oublie! de elbow.
Comment appelez-vous le col?

Alice. De neck, madame.   30

Katherine. De nick.   Et le menton?

Alice. De chin.

Katherine. De sin.   Le col, de nick; de menton, de sin.

Alice. Oui.   Sauf votre honneur, en vérité, vous prononcez les mots aussi droit que les natifs d'Angleterre.

Katherine. Je ne doute point d'apprendre, par la grace de Dieu, et en peu de temps.

Alice. N'avez vous pas déjà oublié ce que je vous ai enseigné?

Katherine. Non, je reciterai à vous promptement: de hand, de fingres, de mails,— 41

Alice. De nails, madame.

Katherine. De nails, de arm, de ilbow.

Alice. Sauf votre honneur, de elbow.

Katherine. Ainsi dis-je; de elbow, de nick, et de sin.   Comment appelez-vous le pied et la robe?

Alice. De foot, madame; et de coun.

Katherine. De foot et de coun!   O Seigneur Dieu! ce sont mots de son mauvais, corruptible, gros, et impudique, et non pour les dames d'honneur d'user: je ne voudrais prononcer ces mots devant les seigneurs de France pour tout le monde. Foh! le foot et le coun!   Néanmoins, je reciterai une autre fois ma leçon ensemble: de hand, de fingres, de nails, de arm, de elbow, de nick, de sin, de foot, de coun. 54

Alice. Excellent, madame!

Katherine. C'est assez pour une fois: allons-nous à dîner.

[*Exeunt.*

SCENE V.   *The Same.*

Enter the KING OF FRANCE, *the* DAUPHIN, *the* DUKE OF BOURBON, *the* CONSTABLE OF FRANCE, *and others.*

French King. 'T is certain he hath pass'd the river Somme.

Constable. And if he be not fought withal, my lord,
Let us not live in France; let us quit all,
And give our vineyards to a barbarous people.

Dauphin. O Dieu vivant! shall a few sprays of us,
The emptying of our fathers' luxury,
Our scions, put in wild and savage stock,
Spirt up so suddenly into the clouds,
And overlook their grafters?
    Bourbon. Normans, but bastard Normans, Norman bas
        tards!   14
Mort de ma vie! if they march along
Unfought withal, but I will sell my dukedom,
To buy a slobbery and a dirty farm
In that nook-shotten isle of Albion.
    Constable. Dieu de batailles! where have they this mettle?
Is not their climate foggy, raw, and dull,
On whom, as in despite, the sun looks pale,
Killing their fruit with frowns? Can sodden water,
A drench for sur-rein'd jades, their barley broth,
Decoct their cold blood to such valiant heat?   20
And shall our quick blood, spirited with wine,
Seem frosty? O, for honour of our land,
Let us not hang like roping icicles
Upon our houses' thatch, whiles a more frosty people
Sweat drops of gallant youth in our rich fields!
Poor we may call them in their native lords.
    Dauphin. By faith and honour,
Our madams mock at us, and plainly say
Our mettle is bred out.
    Bourbon. They bid us to the English dancing-schools, 30
And teach lavoltas high and swift corantos;
Saying our grace is only in our heels,
And that we are most lofty runaways.
    French King. Where is Montjoy the herald? speed him
        hence:
Let him greet England with our sharp defiance.—
Up, princes! and, with spirit of honour edg'd
More sharper than your swords, hie to the field:

that Fortune is plind; and she is painted also with a wheel,
to signify to you, which is the moral of it, that she is turning,
and inconstant, and mutability, and variation: and her foot,
look you, is fixed upon a spherical stone, which rolls, and
rolls, and rolls.   In good truth, the poet makes a most excellent description of it: Fortune is an excellent moral.   35

Pistol. Fortune is Bardolph's foe, and frowns on him;
For he hath stolen a pax, and hanged must a' be:
A damned death!
Let gallows gape for dog; let man go free
And let not hemp his windpipe suffocate:
But Exeter hath given the doom of death
For pax of little price.
Therefore, go speak: the duke will hear thy voice;
And let not Bardolph's vital thread be cut
With edge of penny cord and vile reproach: 45
Speak, captain, for his life, and I will thee requite.

Fluellen. Aunchient Pistol, I do partly understand your
meaning.

Pistol. Why then, rejoice therefore.

Fluellen. Certainly, aunchient, it is not a thing to rejoice
at; for if, look you, he were my prother, I would desire the
duke to use his goot pleasure, and put him to execution; for
discipline ought to pe used.   53

Pistol. Die and be damn'd! and figo for thy friendship!

Fluellen. It is well.

Pistol. The fig of Spain!   [*Exit.*

Fluellen. Very goot.

Gower. Why, this is an arrant counterfeit rascal; I remember him now; a bawd, a cutpurse.

Fluellen. I'll assure you, a' uttered as prave words at the
pridge as you shall see in a summer's day.   But it is very
well; what he has spoke to me, that is well, I warrant you,
when time is serve.   63

Gower. Why, 't is a gull, a fool, a rogue, that now and then

goes to the wars, to grace himself at his return into London
under the form of a soldier. And such fellows are perfect
in the great commanders' names: and they will learn you by
rote where services were done; at such and such a sconce,
at such a breach, at such a convoy; who came off bravely,
who was shot, who disgraced, what terms the enemy stood
on; and this they con perfectly in the phrase of war, which
they trick up with new-tuned oaths: and what a beard of the
general's cut and a horrid suit of the camp will do among
foaming bottles and ale-washed wits, is wonderful to be
thought on. But you must learn to know such slanders of
the age, or else you may be marvellously mistook.   76

Fluellen. I tell you what, Captain Gower; I do perceive
he is not the man that he would gladly make show to the
world he is: if I find a hole in his coat, I will tell him my
mind. [*Drum heard.*] Hark you, the king is coming, and
I must speak with him from the pridge.   81

Drum and colours. Enter KING HENRY, GLOUCESTER,
and Soldiers.

Got pless your majesty!

King Henry. How now, Fluellen! camest thou from the
bridge?

Fluellen. Ay, so please your majesty. The Duke of Exeter
has very gallantly maintained the pridge: the French is gone
off, look you: and there is gallant and most prave passages;
marry, th' athversary was have possession of the pridge; but
he is enforced to retire, and the Duke of Exeter is master of
the pridge: I can tell your majesty, the duke is a prave
man.   90

King Henry. What men have you lost, Fluellen?

Fluellen. The perdition of th' athversary hath peen very
great, reasonable great: marry, for my part, I think the duke
hath lost never a man, but one that is like to pe executed for
robbing a church, one Bardolph, if your majesty know the

man: his face is all bubukles, and whelks, and knobs, and
flames o' fire: and his lips plows at his nose, and it is like
a coal of fire, sometimes plue and sometimes red; but his
nose is executed, and his fire 's out.   99

King Henry. We would have all such offenders so cut off:
and we give express charge, that in our marches through the
country, there be nothing compelled from the villages, nothing taken but paid for, none of the French upbraided or
abused in disdainful language; for when lenity and cruelty
play for a kingdom, the gentler gamester is the soonest
winner.   106

Tucket. Enter MONTJOY.

Montjoy. You know me by my habit.
King Henry. Well then, I know thee: what shall I know
   of thee?
Montjoy. My master's mind.
King Henry. Unfold it.   110
Montjoy. Thus says my king: Say thou to Harry of England: Though we seemed dead, we did but sleep: advantage
is a better soldier than rashness. Tell him we could have
rebuked him at Harfleur, but that we thought not good to
bruise an injury till it were full ripe: now we speak upon our
cue, and our voice is imperial. England shall repent his
folly, see his weakness, and admire our sufferance. Bid him
therefore consider of his ransom; which must proportion the
losses we have borne, the subjects we have lost, the disgrace
we have digested; which in weight to re-answer, his petti-
ness would bow under. For our losses, his exchequer is too
poor; for the effusion of our blood, the muster of his kingdom too faint a number; and for our disgrace, his own person, kneeling at our feet, but a weak and worthless satisfaction. To this add defiance: and tell him, for conclusion,
he hath betrayed his followers, whose condemnation is pronounced. So far my king and master; so much my office.

King Henry. What is thy name?   I know thy quality.
Montjoy. Montjoy.
   King Henry. Thou dost thy office fairly.   Turn thee back,
And tell thy king I do not seek him now;   131
But could be willing to march on to Calais
Without impeachment; for, to say the sooth,
Though 't is no wisdom to confess so much
Unto an enemy of craft and vantage,
My people are with sickness much enfeebled,
My numbers lessen'd, and those few I have
Almost no better than so many French;
Who when they were in health, I tell thee, herald,
I thought upon one pair of English legs   140
Did march three Frenchmen.—Yet, forgive me, God,
That I do brag thus!—This your air of France
Hath blown that vice in me; I must repent.
Go therefore, tell thy master here I am:
My ransom is this frail and worthless trunk,
My army but a weak and sickly guard;
Yet, God before, tell him we will come on,
Though France himself and such another neighbour
Stand in our way.   There 's for thy labour, Montjoy.
Go, bid thy master well advise himself: 150
If we may pass, we will; if we be hinder'd,
We shall your tawny ground with your red blood
Discolour: and so, Montjoy, fare you well.
The sum of all our answer is but this:
We would not seek a battle, as we are,
Nor, as we are, we say we will not shun it:
So tell your master.
   Montjoy. I shall deliver so.   Thanks to your highness.
                                            [*Exit.*

   Gloucester. I hope they will not come upon us now.
   King Henry. We are in God's hand, brother, not in
        theirs.

March to the bridge; it now draws toward night.   161
Beyond the river we 'll encamp ourselves,
And on to-morrow bid them march away.   [*Exeunt.*

Scene VII.   *The French Camp, near Agincourt.*

Enter the Constable of France, *the* Lord Rambures,
Orleans, Dauphin, *with others.*

Constable. Tut! I have the best armour of the world.
Would it were day!

Orleans. You have an excellent armour; but let my
horse have his due.

Constable. It is the best horse of Europe.

Orleans. Will it never be morning?

Dauphin. My Lord of Orleans, and my lord high constable, you talk of horse and armour?

Orleans. You are as well provided of both as any prince
in the world.   10

Dauphin. What a long night is this!—I will not change
my horse with any that treads but on four pasterns.   Ça, ha!
he bounds from the earth, as if his entrails were hairs; le
cheval volant, the Pegasus, chez les narines de feu! When
I bestride him, I soar, I am a hawk: he trots the air; the
earth sings when he touches it; the basest horn of his
hoof is more musical than the pipe of Hermes.

Orleans. He 's of the colour of the nutmeg.

Dauphin. And of the heat of the ginger.   It is a beast for
Perseus: he is pure air and fire; and the dull elements of
earth and water never appear in him, but only in patient
stillness while his rider mounts him: he is indeed a horse;
and all other jades you may call beasts.   23

Constable. Indeed, my lord, it is a most absolute and excellent horse.

Dauphin. It is the prince of palfreys; his neigh is like the
bidding of a monarch, and his countenance enforces homage.

Orleans. No more, cousin.

Dauphin. Nay, the man hath no wit that cannot, from the rising of the lark to the lodging of the lamb, vary deserved praise on my palfrey: it is a theme as fluent as the sea: turn the sands into eloquent tongues, and my horse is argument for them all. 'T is a subject for a sovereign to reason on, and for a sovereign's sovereign to ride on; and for the world, familiar to us and unknown, to lay apart their particular functions and wonder at him. I once writ a sonnet in his praise and began thus: 'Wonder of nature,'—   37

Orleans. I have heard a sonnet begin so to one's mistress.

Dauphin. Then did they imitate that which I composed to my courser, for my horse is my mistress.

Orleans. Your mistress bears well.

Dauphin. Me well; which is the prescript praise and perfection of a good and particular mistress.

Constable. Nay, for methought yesterday your mistress shrewdly shook your back.   45

Dauphin. So perhaps did yours.

Dauphin. I tell thee, constable, my mistress wears his own hair.

Constable. I could make as true a boast as that, if I had a sow to my mistress.   50

Dauphin. 'Le chien est retourné à son propre vomissement, et la truie lavée au bourbier:' thou makest use of any thing.

Constable. Yet do I not use my horse for my mistress, or any such proverb so little kin to the purpose.

Rambures. My lord constable, the armour that I saw in your tent to-night, are those stars or suns upon it?

Constable. Stars, my lord.

Dauphin. Some of them will fall to-morrow, I hope.

Constable. And yet my sky shall not want.   60

Dauphin. That may be, for you bear a many superfluously, and 't were more honour some were away.

Constable. Even as your horse bears your praises; who would trot as well, were some of your brags dismounted.

Dauphin. Would I were able to load him with his desert! —Will it never be day? I will trot to-morrow a mile, and my way shall be paved with English faces.

Constable. I will not say so, for fear I should be faced out of my way: but I would it were morning; for I would fain be about the ears of the English. 70

Rambures. Who will go to hazard with me for twenty prisoners?

Constable. You must first go yourself to hazard, ere you have them.

Dauphin. 'T is midnight; I 'll go arm myself. [*Exit.*

Orleans. The Dauphin longs for morning.

Rambures. He longs to eat the English.

Constable. I think he will eat all he kills.

Orleans. By the white hand of my lady, he 's a gallant prince. 80

Constable. Swear by her foot, that she may tread out the oath.

Orleans. He is simply the most active gentleman of France.

Constable. Doing is activity; and he will still be doing.

Orleans. He never did harm, that I heard of.

Constable. Nor will do none to-morrow: he will keep that good name still.

Orleans. I know him to be valiant.

Constable. I was told that by one that knows him better than you. 91

Orleans. What 's he?

Constable. Marry, he told me so himself; and he said he cared not who knew it.

Orleans. He needs not; it is no hidden virtue in him.

Constable. By my faith, sir, but it is; never any body saw it but his lackey: 't is a hooded valour, and when it appears it will bate.

Orleans. Ill will never said well.

Constable. I will cap that proverb with 'There is flattery in friendship.' 101

Orleans. And I will take up that with 'Give the devil his due.'

Constable. Well placed: there stands your friend for the devil: have at the very eye of that proverb with 'A pox of the devil.'

Orleans. You are the better at proverbs, by how much 'A fool's bolt is soon shot.'

Constable. You have shot over.

Orleans. 'T is not the first time you were overshot. 110

Enter a Messenger.

Messenger. My lord high constable, the English lie within fifteen hundred paces of your tents.

Constable. Who hath measured the ground?

Messenger. The Lord Grandpré.

Constable. A valiant and most expert gentleman.—Would it were day!—Alas, poor Harry of England! he longs not for the dawning as we do.

Orleans. What a wretched and peevish fellow is this king of England, to mope with his fat-brained followers so far out of his knowledge! 120

Constable. If the English had any apprehension, they would run away.

Orleans. That they lack; for if their heads had any intellectual armour, they could never wear such heavy head-pieces.

Rambures. That island of England breeds very valiant creatures; their mastiffs are of unmatchable courage.

Orleans. Foolish curs, that run winking into the mouth of a Russian bear and have their heads crushed like rotten apples! You may as well say, that's a valiant flea that dare eat his breakfast on the lip of a lion. 130

Constable. Just, just; and the men do sympathize with the mastiffs in robustious and rough coming on, leaving their wits with their wives: and then give them great meals of beef and iron and steel, they will eat like wolves and fight like devils.

Orleans. Ay, but these English are shrewdly out of beef.

Constable. Then shall we find to-morrow they have only stomachs to eat, and none to fight.   Now is it time to arm: come, shall we about it?   139

Orleans. It is now two o'clock: but, let me see, by ten
We shall have each a hundred Englishmen.   [*Exeunt.*

And giddy Fortune's furious fickle wheel,
That goddess blind,
That stands upon the rolling restless stone (iii. 6. 25).

THE FIELD OF AGINCOURT.

ACT IV.

PROLOGUE.

Enter Chorus.

Chorus. Now entertain conjecture of a time
When creeping murmur and the poring dark
Fills the wide vessel of the universe.
From camp to camp through the foul womb of night
The hum of either army stilly sounds,
That the fix'd sentinels almost receive

The secret whispers of each other's watch.
Fire answers fire, and through their paly flames
Each battle sees the other's umber'd face:
Steed threatens steed, in high and boastful neighs   10
Piercing the night's dull ear; and from the tents
The armourers, accomplishing the knights,
With busy hammers closing rivets up,
Give dreadful note of preparation:
The country cocks do crow, the clocks do toll,
And the third hour of drowsy morning name.
Proud of their numbers and secure in soul,
The confident and over-lusty French
Do the low-rated English play at dice;
And chide the cripple tardy-gaited night,   20
Who, like a foul and ugly witch, doth limp
So tediously away.   The poor condemned English,
Like sacrifices, by their watchful fires
Sit patiently, and inly ruminate
The morning's danger; and their gesture sad,
Investing lank-lean cheeks and war-worn coats,
Presenteth them unto the gazing moon
So many horrid ghosts.   O now, who will behold
The royal captain of this ruin'd band
Walking from watch to watch, from tent to tent,   30
Let him cry ' Praise and glory on his head !'
For forth he goes and visits all his host,
Bids them good morrow with a modest smile,
And calls them brothers, friends, and countrymen.
Upon his royal face there is no note
How dread an army hath enrounded him;
Nor doth he dedicate one jot of colour
Unto the weary and all-watched night,
But freshly looks, and over-bears attaint
With cheerful semblance and sweet majesty;   40
That every wretch, pining and pale before,

F

Beholding him, plucks comfort from his looks:
A largess universal like the sun
His liberal eye doth give to every one,
Thawing cold fear.   Then, mean and gentle all,
Behold, as may unworthiness define,
A little touch of Harry in the night.
And so our scene must to the battle fly;
Where—O for pity!—we shall much disgrace
With four or five most vile and ragged foils,   50
Right ill-dispos'd in brawl ridiculous,
The name of Agincourt.   Yet sit and see,
Minding true things by what their mockeries be.   [*Exit.*

SCENE I. *The English Camp at Agincourt.*

Enter KING HENRY, BEDFORD, *and* GLOUCESTER.

King Henry. Gloucester, 't is true that we are in great
        danger;
The greater therefore should our courage be.—
Good morrow, brother Bedford.—God Almighty!
There is some soul of goodness in things evil,
Would men observingly distil it out;
For our bad neighbour makes us early stirrers,
Which is both healthful and good husbandry:
Besides, they are our outward consciences,
And preachers to us all, admonishing
That we should dress us fairly for our end.   10
Thus may we gather honey from the weed,
And make a moral of the devil himself.

Enter ERPINGHAM.

Good morrow, old Sir Thomas Erpingham:
A good soft pillow for that good white head
Were better than a churlish turf of France.
        Erpingham. Not so, my liege: this lodging likes me better.
Since I may say, now lie I like a king.

King Henry. 'T is good for men to love their present
 pains
Upon example ; so the spirit is eas'd :
And when the mind is quicken'd, out of doubt,   20
The organs, though defunct and dead before,
Break up their drowsy grave and newly move,
With casted slough and fresh legerity.
Lend me thy cloak, Sir Thomas.—Brothers **both,**
Commend me to the princes in our **camp ;**
Do my good morrow to them, and **anon**
Desire them all to my pavilion.
 Gloucester. We shall, my liege.
 Erpingham. Shall I attend your **grace ?**
 King Henry.   **No, my** good knight ;
Go with my brothers to my lords of **England :** 30
I and my bosom must debate a while,
And then I would no other company.
 Erpingham. The Lord in heaven **bless thee,** noble Harry !
        [*Exeunt all but King.*
 King Henry. God-a-mercy, old heart ! **thou speak'st** cheer-
 fully.

Enter PISTOL.

 Pistol. Qui va là ?
 King Henry. A friend.
 Pistol. Discuss unto me ; art thou **officer ?**
Or art thou base, common, and popular ?
 King Henry. I am a gentleman of a **company.**
 Pistol. Trail'st thou the puissant pike ?
 King Henry. Even so. What are **you ?**   40
 Pistol. As good a gentleman as the **emperor.**
 King Henry. Then you are a better than the king.
 Pistol. The king 's a bawcock, and **a heart of gold,**
A lad of life, an imp of fame ;
Of parents good, of fist most valiant.

I kiss his dirty shoe, and from heart-strings
I love the lovely bully.   What is thy name?

King Henry. Harry le Roy.

Pistol. Le Roy! a Cornish name: art thou of Cornish
crew?   5c

King Henry. No, I am a Welshman.

Pistol. Know'st thou Fluellen?

King Henry. Yes.

Pistol. Tell him, I'll knock his leek about his pate
Upon Saint Davy's day.

King Henry. Do not you wear your dagger in your cap
that day, lest he knock that about yours.

Pistol. Art thou his friend?

King Henry. And his kinsman too.

Pistol. The figo for thee, then!   6o

King Henry. I thank you: God be with you!

Pistol. My name is Pistol call'd.   [*Exit.*

King Henry. It sorts well with your fierceness.

Enter FLUELLEN *and* GOWER.

Gower. Captain Fluellen!

Fluellen. So! in the name of Cheshu Christ, speak lower.
It is the greatest admiration in the universal world, when the
true and aunchient prerogatifes and laws of the wars is not
kept.   If you would take the pains but to examine the wars
of Pompey the Great, you shall find, I warrant you, that there
is no tiddle taddle nor pibble pabble in Pompey's camp; I
warrant you, you shall find the ceremonies of the wars, and
the cares of it, and the forms of it, and the sobriety of it, and
the modesty of it, to pe otherwise.   73

Gower. Why, the enemy is loud; you hear him all night.

Fluellen. If the enemy is an ass and a fool and a prating
coxcomb, is it meet, think you, that we should also, look you,
pe an ass and a fool and a prating coxcomb? in your own
conscience, now?

Gower. I will speak lower.

Fluellen. I pray you and peseech you that you will.   80
                    [*Exeunt Gower and Fluellen.*

King Henry. Though it appear a little out of fashion,
There is much care and valour in this Welshman.

Enter BATES, COURT, *and* WILLIAMS.

Court. Brother John Bates, is not that the morning which breaks yonder?

Bates. I think it be: but we have no great cause to desire the approach of day.

Williams. We see yonder the beginning of the day, but I think we shall never see the end of it.—Who goes there?

King Henry. A friend.

Williams. Under what captain serve you?   90

King Henry. Under Sir Thomas Erpingham.

Williams. A good old commander and a most kind gentleman: I pray you, what thinks he of our estate?

King Henry. Even as men wracked upon a sand, that look to be washed off the next tide.

Bates. He hath not told his thought to the king?

King Henry. No; nor it is not meet he should. For, though I speak it to you, I think the king is but a man, as I am: the violet smells to him as it doth to me; the element shows to him as it doth to me; all his senses have but human conditions: his ceremonies laid by, in his nakedness he appears but a man; and though his affections are higher mounted than ours, yet, when they stoop, they stoop with the like wing. Therefore when he sees reason of fears, as we do, his fears, out of doubt, be of the same relish as ours are: yet, in reason, no man should possess him with any appearance of fear, lest he, by showing it, should dishearten his army.   108

Bates. He may show what outward courage he will; but I believe, as cold a night as 't is, he could wish himself in

Thames up to the neck; and so I would he were, and I by him, at all adventures, so we were quit here.

King Henry. By my troth, I will speak my conscience of the king: I think he would not wish himself any where but where he is.

Bates. Then I would he were here alone; so should he be sure to be ransomed, and a many poor men's lives saved.

King Henry. I dare say you love him not so ill, to wish him here alone, howsoever you speak this to feel other men's minds. Methinks I could not die any where so contented as in the king's company, his cause being just and his quarrel honourable.   122

Williams. That 's more than we know.

Bates. Ay, or more than we should seek after; for we know enough, if we know we are the king's subjects. If his cause be wrong, our obedience to the king wipes the crime of it out of us.

Williams. But if the cause be not good, the king himself hath a heavy reckoning to make, when all those legs and arms and heads, chopped off in a battle, shall join together at the latter day and cry all ' We died at such a place;' some swearing, some crying for a surgeon, some upon their wives left poor behind them, some upon the debts they owe, some upon their children rawly left. I am afeard there are few die well that die in a battle; for how can they charitably dispose of any thing, when blood is their argument? Now, if these men do not die well, it will be a black matter for the king that led them to it; who to disobey were against all proportion of subjection.   139

King Henry. So, if a son that is by his father sent about merchandise do sinfully miscarry upon the sea, the imputation of his wickedness, by your rule, should be imposed upon his father that sent him; or if a servant, under his master's command transporting a sum of money, be assailed by robbers and die in many irreconciled iniquities, you may call

the business of the master the author of the servant's damnation. But this is not so: the king is not bound to answer
the particular endings of his soldiers, the father of his son,
nor the master of his servant; for they purpose not their
death when they purpose their services. Besides, there is
no king, be his cause never so spotless, if it come to the ar-
bitrement of swords, can try it out with all unspotted soldiers. Some peradventure have on them the guilt of pre-
meditated and contrived murther; some, of beguiling virgins
with the broken seals of perjury; some, making the wars
their bulwark, that have before gored the gentle bosom of
peace with pillage and robbery. Now, if these men have de-
feated the law and outrun native punishment, though they
can outstrip men, they have no wings to fly from God: war
is his beadle, war is his vengeance; so that here men are
punished for before-breach of the king's laws in now the
king's quarrel: where they feared the death, they have borne
life away; and where they would be safe, they perish: then
if they die unprovided, no more is the king guilty of their
damnation than he was before guilty of those impieties for
the which they are now visited. Every subject's duty is the
king's; but every subject's soul is his own. Therefore should
every soldier in the wars do as every sick man in his bed,
wash every mote out of his conscience: and dying so, death
is to him advantage; or not dying, the time was blessedly
lost wherein such preparation was gained: and in him that
escapes, it were not sin to think that, making God so free an
offer, He let him outlive that day to see His greatness and
to teach others how they should prepare.   174

Williams. 'T is certain, every man that dies ill, the ill upon
his own head; the king is not to answer it.

Bates. I do not desire he should answer for me; and yet
I determine to fight lustily for him.

King Henry. I myself heard the king say he would not be
ransomed.   180

Williams. Ay, he said so, to make us fight cheerfully; but when our throats are cut, he may be ransomed, and we ne'er the wiser.

King Henry. If I live to see it, I will never trust his word after.

Williams. You pay him then! That's a perilous shot out of an elder-gun, that a poor and private displeasure can do against a monarch. You may as well go about to turn the sun to ice with fanning in his face with a peacock's feather. You'll never trust his word after! come, 't is a foolish saying.

King Henry. Your reproof is something too round: I should be angry with you, if the time were convenient. 192

Williams. Let it be a quarrel between us, if you live.

King Henry. I embrace it.

Williams. How shall I know thee again?

King Henry. Give me any gage of thine, and I will wear it in my bonnet: then, if ever thou darest acknowledge it, I will make it my quarrel.

Williams. Here's my glove: give me another of thine.

King Henry. There. 200

Williams. This will I also wear in my cap: if ever thou come to me and say, after to-morrow, 'This is my glove,' by this hand, I will take thee a box on the ear.

King Henry. If ever I live to see it, I will challenge it.

Williams. Thou darest as well be hanged.

King Henry. Well, I will do it, though I take thee in the king's company.

Williams. Keep thy word: fare thee well.

Bates. Be friends, you English fools, be friends: we have French quarrels enow, if you could tell how to reckon. 210

King Henry. Indeed, the French may lay twenty French crowns to one, they will beat us; for they bear them on their shoulders: but it is no English treason to cut French crowns, and to-morrow the king himself will be a clipper.

[*Exeunt Soldiers.*

Upon the king! let us our lives, our souls,
Our debts, our careful wives,
Our children, and our sins lay on the king!
We must bear all.   O hard condition,
Twin-born with greatness, subject to the breath
Of every fool, whose sense no more can feel   220
But his own wringing!   What infinite heart's-ease
Must kings neglect, that private men enjoy!
And what have kings, that privates have not too,
Save ceremony, save general ceremony?
And what art thou, thou idol ceremony?
What kind of god art thou, that suffer'st more
Of mortal griefs than do thy worshippers?
What are thy rents? what are thy comings-in?
O ceremony, show me but thy worth!
What is thy soul of adoration?   230
Art thou aught else but place, degree, and form,
Creating awe and fear in other men?
Wherein thou art less happy being fear'd
Than they in fearing.
What drink'st thou oft, instead of homage sweet,
But poison'd flattery?   O, be sick, great greatness,
And bid thy ceremony give thee cure!
Think'st thou the fiery fever will go out
With titles blown from adulation?
Will it give place to flexure and low bending?   240
Canst thou, when thou command'st the beggar's knee,
Command the health of it?   No, thou proud dream,
That play'st so subtly with a king's repose;
I am a king that find thee, and I know
'T is not the balm, the sceptre, and the ball,
The sword, the mace, the crown imperial,
The intertissued robe of gold and pearl,
The farced title running fore the king,
The throne he sits on, nor the tide of pomp

That beats upon the high shore of this world;   250
No, not all these, thrice-gorgeous ceremony,
Not all these, laid in bed majestical,
Can sleep so soundly as the wretched slave,
Who with a body fill'd and vacant mind
Gets him to rest, cramm'd with distressful bread,
Never sees horrid night, the child of hell,
But, like a lackey, from the rise to set
Sweats in the eye of Phœbus, and all night
Sleeps in Elysium; next day after dawn,
Doth rise and help Hyperion to his horse,   260
And follows so the ever-running year,
With profitable labour, to his grave:
And, but for ceremony, such a wretch,
Winding up days with toil and nights with sleep,
Had the fore-hand and vantage of a king.
The slave, a member of the country's peace,
Enjoys it, but in gross brain little wots
What watch the king keeps to maintain the peace,
Whose hours the peasant best advantages.

Enter ERPINGHAM.

   Erpingham. My lord, your nobles, jealous of your absence,
Seek through your camp to find you.
   King Henry.   Good old knight,   271
Collect them all together at my tent:
I 'll be before thee.
   Erpingham.   I shall do 't, my lord.   [*Exit.*
   King Henry. O God of battles! steel my soldiers' hearts;
Possess them not with fear; take from them now
The sense of reckoning, if the opposed numbers
Pluck their hearts from them.   Not to-day, O Lord,
O, not to-day, think not upon the fault
My father made in compassing the crown!
I Richard's body have interred new,   280

And on it have bestow'd more contrite tears
Than from it issued forced drops of blood.
Five hundred poor I have in yearly pay,
Who twice a-day their wither'd hands hold up
Toward heaven, to pardon blood; and I have built
Two chantries, where the sad and solemn priests
Sing still for Richard's soul.   More will I do;
Though all that I can do is nothing worth,
Since that my penitence comes after all,
Imploring pardon.   290

Enter GLOUCESTER.

Gloucester. My liege!
King Henry. My brother Gloucester's voice?   Ay;
I know thy errand, I will go with thee:
The day, my friends, and all things stay for me.   [*Exeunt.*

SCENE II.   *The French Camp.*

Enter the DAUPHIN, ORLEANS, RAMBURES, *and others.*

Orleans. The sun doth gild our armour; up, my lords!
Dauphin. Montez à cheval!   My horse! varlet! laquais!
      ha!
Orleans. O brave spirit!
Dauphin. Via! les eaux et la terre.
Orleans. Rien puis? l'air et le feu.
Dauphin. Ciel, cousin Orleans.

Enter CONSTABLE.

Now, my lord constable!
      Constable. Hark, how our steeds for present service
            neigh!
      Dauphin. Mount them, and make incision in their hides,
That their hot blood may spin in English eyes,   10
And dout them with superfluous courage, ha!

Rambures. What, will you have them weep our horses'
    blood?
How shall we then behold their natural tears?

Enter Messenger.

Messenger. The English are embattled, you French peers.
Constable. To horse, you gallant princes! straight to horse!
Do but behold yon poor and starved band,
And your fair show shall suck away their souls,
Leaving them but the shales and husks of men.
There is not work enough for all our hands;
Scarce blood enough in all their sickly veins   20
To give each naked curtle-axe a stain,
That our French gallants shall to-day draw out,
And sheathe for lack of sport: let us but blow on them,
The vapour of our valour will o'erturn them.
'T is positive 'gainst all exceptions, lords,
That our superfluous lackeys and our peasants,
Who in unnecessary action swarm
About our squares of battle, were enow
To purge this field of such a hilding foe,
Though we upon this mountain's basis by   30
Took stand for idle speculation:
But that our honours must not.   What 's to say?
A very little little let us do,
And all is done.   Then let the trumpets sound
The tucket sonance and the note to mount;
For our approach shall so much dare the field
That England shall couch down in fear and yield.

Enter GRANDPRÉ.

Grandpré. Why do you stay so long, my lords of France?
Yon island carrions, desperate of their bones,
Ill-favouredly become the morning field: 40
Their ragged curtains poorly are let loose,

And our air shakes them passing scornfully:
Big Mars seems bankrupt in their beggar'd host,
And faintly through a rusty beaver peeps:
The horsemen sit like fixed candlesticks,
With torch-staves in their hand; and their poor jades
Lob down their heads, dropping the hides and hips,
The gum down-roping from their pale-dead eyes,
And in their pale dull mouths the gimmal bit
Lies foul with chew'd grass, still and motionless;   50
And their executors, the knavish crows,
Fly o'er them, all impatient for their hour.
Description cannot suit itself in words
To demonstrate the life of such a battle,
'n life so lifeless as it shows itself.

   Constable. They have said their prayers, and they stay for
      death.

   Dauphin. Shall we go send them dinners and fresh suits,
And give their fasting horses provender,
And after fight with them?

   Constable. I stay but for my guidon: to the field!   60
I will the banner from a trumpet take,
And use it for my haste. Come, come, away!
The sun is high, and we outwear the day.   *[Exeunt.*

SCENE III. *The English Camp.*

Enter the English Host; GLOUCESTER, BEDFORD, EXETER,
   ERPINGHAM, SALISBURY, *and* WESTMORELAND.

Gloucester. Where is the king?

Bedford. The king himself is rode to view their battle.

Westmoreland. Of fighting men they have full threescore
    thousand.

Exeter. There's five to one; besides, they all are fresh.

Salisbury. God's arm strike with us! 't is a fearful odds.

God be wi' you, princes all; I 'll to my charge:

If we no more meet till we meet in heaven,
Then, joyfully, my noble Lord of Bedford,
My dear Lord Gloucester, and my good Lord **Exeter,**
And my kind kinsman, warriors all, adieu !   10

    Bedford. Farewell, good Salisbury ; and good luck go with
      thee !

    Exeter. Farewell, kind lord ; fight valiantly to-day :
And yet I do thee wrong to mind thee of it,
For thou art fram'd of the firm truth of valour.

                              [Exit Salisbury.

    Bedford. He is as full of valour as of kindness ;
Princely in both.

                Enter the KING.

    Westmoreland.   O that we now had here
But one ten thousand of those men in England
That do no work to-day !

    King Henry.   What 's he that wishes so ?
My cousin Westmoreland ?   No, my fair cousin :
If we are mark'd to die, we are enow   20
To do our country loss ; and if to live,
The fewer men, the greater share of honour.
God's will ! I pray thee, wish not one man more.
By Jove, I am not covetous for gold,
Nor care I who doth feed upon my cost ;
It yearns me not if men my garments wear ;
Such outward things dwell not in my desires :
But if it be a sin to covet honour,
I am the most offending soul alive.
No, faith, my coz, wish not a man from England :   30
God's peace ! I would not lose so great an honour
As one man more, methinks, would share from me
For the best hope I have.   O, do not wish one more !
Rather proclaim it, Westmoreland, through my host,
That he which hath no stomach to this fight,

Let him depart; his passport shall be made,
And crowns for convoy put into his purse:
We would not die in that man's company
That fears his fellowship to die with us.
This day is call'd the feast of Crispian: 40
He that outlives this day, and comes safe home,
Will stand a tip-toe when this day is nam'd,
And rouse him at the name of Crispian.
He that shall live this day, and see old age,
Will yearly on the vigil feast his neighbours,
And say 'To-morrow is Saint Crispian:'
Then will he strip his sleeve and show his scars,
And say 'These wounds I had on Crispin's day.'
Old men forget; yet all shall be forgot,
But he'll remember with advantages   50
What feats he did that day: then shall our names,
Familiar in his mouth as household words,—
Harry the king, Bedford and Exeter,
Warwick and Talbot, Salisbury and Gloucester,—
Be in their flowing cups freshly remember'd.
This story shall the good man teach his son;
And Crispin Crispian shall ne'er go by,
From this day to the ending of the world,
But we in it shall be remembered,
We few, we happy few, we band of brothers: 60
For he to-day that sheds his blood with me
Shall be my brother; be he ne'er so vile,
This day shall gentle his condition:
And gentlemen in England now a-bed
Shall think themselves accurs'd they were not here,
And hold their manhoods cheap whiles any speaks
That fought with us upon Saint Crispin's day.

Enter SALISBURY.

Salisbury. My sovereign lord, bestow yourself with speed:

The French are bravely in their battles set,
And will with all expedience charge on us.   70
> *King Henry.* All things are ready, if our minds be so.
> *Westmoreland.* Perish the man whose mind is backward
> now!
> *King Henry.* Thou dost not wish more help from Eng-
> land, coz?
> *Westmoreland.* God's will! my liege, would you and I
> alone,
Without more help, could fight this royal battle!
> *King Henry.* Why, now thou hast unwish'd five thousand
> men,
Which likes me better than to wish us one.—
You know your places: God be with you all!

Tucket.   Enter MONTJOY.

> *Montjoy.* Once more I come to know of thee, King Harry,
If for thy ransom thou wilt now compound,   80
Before thy most assured overthrow:
For certainly thou art so near the gulf,
Thou needs must be englutted.   Besides, in mercy,
The constable desires thee thou wilt mind
Thy followers of repentance; that their souls
May make a peaceful and a sweet retire
From off these fields, where, wretches, their poor bodies
Must lie and fester.
> *King Henry.*   Who hath sent thee now?
> *Montjoy.* The Constable of France.
> *King Henry.* I pray thee, bear my former answer back:
Bid them achieve me, and then sell my bones.   91
Good God! why should they mock poor fellows thus?
The man that once did sell the lion's skin
While the beast liv'd was kill'd with hunting him.
A many of our bodies shall no doubt
Find native graves; upon the which, I trust,

Shall witness live in brass of this day's work;
And those that leave their valiant bones in France,
Dying like men, though buried in your dunghills,
They shall be fam'd: for there the sun shall greet
  them,   100
And draw their honours reeking up to heaven,
Leaving their earthly parts to choke your clime,
The smell whereof shall breed a plague in France.
Mark then abounding valour in our English,
That, being dead, like to the bullet's grazing,
Break out into a second course of mischief,
Killing in relapse of mortality.
Let me speak proudly: tell the constable
We are but warriors for the working-day;
Our gayness and our gilt are all besmirch'd   110
With rainy marching in the painful field;
There's not a piece of feather in our host—
Good argument, I hope, we will not fly—
And time hath worn us into slovenry:
But, by the mass, our hearts are in the trim;
And my poor soldiers tell me, yet ere night
They 'll be in fresher robes, or they will pluck
The gay new coats o'er the French soldiers' heads,
And turn them out of service. If they do this,—
As, if God please, they shall,—my ransom then 120
Will soon be levied. Herald, save thou thy labour;
Come thou no more for ransom, gentle herald:
They shall have none, I swear, but these my joints;
Which if they have as I will leave 'em them,
Shall yield them little, tell the constable.

 Montjoy. I shall, King Harry. And so fare thee well:
Thou never shalt hear herald any more.   [*Exit.*

 King Henry. I fear thou 'lt once more come again for
  ransom.

         G

Enter York.

York. My lord, most humbly on my knee **I beg**
The leading of the vaward.   130
    King Henry. Take it, brave York.—Now, soldiers, march
      away:
And how thou pleasest, God, dispose the day!   [*Exeunt.*

Scene IV. *The Field of Battle.*

Alarum. Excursions. Enter French Soldier, Pistol, *and*
Boy.

    Pistol. Yield, cur!
    French Soldier. Je pense que vous êtes gentilhomme de
bonne qualité.
    Pistol. Quality! Callino, castore me! Art thou a gentle
man? what is thy name? discuss.
    French Soldier. O Seigneur Dieu!
    Pistol. O, Signieur Dew should be a gentleman:
Perpend my words, O Signieur Dew, and mark;
O Signieur Dew, thou diest on point of fox,
Except, O signieur, thou do give to me   10
Egregious ransom.
    French Soldier. O, prenez miséricorde! ayez pitié de
moi!
    Pistol. Moy shall not serve, I will have forty moys;
Or I will fetch thy rim out at thy throat
In drops of crimson blood.
    French Soldier. Est-il impossible d'échapper la force de
ton bras?
    Pistol. Brass, cur!
Thou damned and luxurious mountain goat,   20
Offer'st me brass?
    French Soldier. O pardonnez moi!
    Pistol. Say'st thou me so? is that a ton of moys?

Come hither, boy: ask me this slave in French
What is his name.

Boy. Écoutez: comment êtes-vous appelé?

French Soldier. Monsieur le Fer.

Boy. He says his name is Master Fer.

Pistol. Master Fer! I 'll fer him, and firk him, and ferret
him: discuss the same in French unto him.   30

Boy. I do not know the French for fer, and ferret, and
firk.

Pistol. Bid him prepare; for I will cut his throat.

French Soldier. Que dit-il, monsieur?

Boy. Il me commande de vous dire que vous faites vous
prêt; car ce soldat ici est disposé tout à cette heure de
couper votre gorge.

Pistol. Owy, cuppele gorge, permafoy,
Peasant, unless thou give me crowns, brave crowns;
Or mangled shalt thou be by this my sword.   40

French Soldier. O, je vous supplie, pour l'amour de Dieu,
me pardonner! Je suis gentilhomme de bonne maison: gar-
dez ma vie, et je vous donnerai deux cents écus.

Pistol. What are his words?

Boy. He prays you to save his life: he is a gentleman of
a good house; and for his ransom he will give you two hundred crowns.

Pistol. Tell him my fury shall abate, and I
The crowns will take.

French Soldier. Petit monsieur, que dit-il?   50

Boy. Encore qu'il est contre son jurement de pardonner
aucun prisonnier, néanmoins, pour les écus que vous l'avez
promis, il est content de vous donner la liberté, le franchise-
ment.

French Soldier. Sur mes genoux je vous donne mille re-
mercîmens; et je m'estime heureux que je suis tombé entre
les mains d'un chevalier, je pense, le plus brave, vaillant, et
très distingué seigneur d'Angleterre.

Pistol. Expound unto me, boy.

Boy. He gives you, upon his knees, a thousand thanks; and he esteems himself happy that he hath fallen into the hands of one, as he thinks, the most brave, valorous, and thrice-worthy signieur of England. 63

Pistol. As I suck blood, I will some mercy show. Follow me!

Boy. Suivez-vous le grand capitaine. [*Exeunt Pistol and French Soldier.*] I did never know so full a voice issue from so empty a heart: but the saying is true, 'The empty vessel makes the greatest sound.' Bardolph and Nym had ten times more valour than this roaring devil i' the old play, that every one may pare his nails with a wooden dagger; and they are both hanged; and so would this be, if he durst steal any thing adventurously. I must stay with the lackeys, with the luggage of our camp: the French might have a good prey of us, if he knew of it; for there is none to guard it but boys. [*Exit.*

SCENE V. *Another Part of the Field.*

Enter ORLEANS, BOURBON, DAUPHIN, CONSTABLE, *and* RAMBURES.

Constable. O diable!

Orleans. O Seigneur! le jour est perdu, tout est perdu!

Dauphin. Mort de ma vie! all is confounded, all!
Reproach and everlasting shame
Sits mocking in our plumes. O méchante fortune!
Do not run away. [*A short alarum.*

Constable. Why, all our ranks are broke.

Dauphin. O perdurable shame! let 's stab ourselves.
Be these the wretches that we play'd at dice for?

Orleans. Is this the king we sent to for his ransom?

Bourbon. Shame and eternal shame, nothing but shame!
Let us die in honour: once more back again! 11

Constable. Disorder, that hath spoil'd us, friend us **now!**
Let us on heaps go offer up our lives.

Orleans. We are enow yet living in the field
To smother up the English in our throngs,
If any order might be thought upon.

Bourbon. The devil take order now! I 'll to the throng:
Let life be short; else shame will be too long.   [*Exeunt.*

SCENE VI.   *Another Part of the Field.*

Alarums.   Enter KING HENRY *and forces,* EXETER, *and
others.*

King Henry. Well have we done, thrice valiant countrymen:
But all 's not done; yet keep the French the field.

Exeter. The Duke of York commends him to your majesty.

King Henry. Lives he, good uncle? thrice within this hour
I saw him down, thrice up again, and fighting;
From helmet to the spur all blood he was.

Exeter. In which array, brave soldier, doth he lie,
Larding the plain; and by his bloody side,
Yoke-fellow to his honour-owing wounds,
The noble Earl of Suffolk also lies.   10
Suffolk first died: and York, all haggled over,
Comes to him, where in gore he lay insteep'd,
And takes him by the beard, kisses the gashes
That bloodily did yawn upon his face,
And cries aloud 'Tarry, dear cousin Suffolk!
My soul shall thine keep company to heaven;
Tarry, sweet soul, for mine, then fly abreast,
As in this glorious and well-foughten field
We kept together in our chivalry!'
Upon these words I came and cheer'd him up: 20
He smil'd me in the face, raught me his hand,

And, with a feeble gripe, says 'Dear my lord,
Commend my service to my sovereign.'
So did he turn, and over Suffolk's neck
He threw his wounded arm, and kiss'd his lips;
And so espous'd to death, with blood he seal'd
A testament of noble-ending love.
The pretty and sweet manner of it forc'd
Those waters from me which I would have stopp'd;
But I had not so much of man in me,   30
And all my mother came into mine eyes
And gave me up to tears.

   King Henry.   I blame you not;
For, hearing this, I must perforce compound
With mistful eyes, or they will issue too.—   [*Alarum.*
But, hark! what new alarum is this same?
The French have reinforc'd their scatter'd men:
Then every soldier kill his prisoners;
Give the word through.   [*Exeunt.*

SCENE VII. *Another Part of the Field.*

Enter FLUELLEN *and* GOWER.

Fluellen. Kill the poys and the luggage! 't is expressly
against the law of arms: 't is as arrant a piece of knavery,
mark you now, as can pe offert; in your conscience, now,
is it not?

Gower. 'T is certain there 's not a boy left alive; and
the cowardly rascals that ran from the battle ha' done this
slaughter; besides, they have burned and carried away all
that was in the king's tent; wherefore the king, most worthily, hath caused every soldier to cut his prisoner's throat.
O, 't is a gallant king!   10

Fluellen. Ay, he was porn at Monmouth, Captain Gower.
What call you the town's name where Alexander the Pig
was porn?

Gower. Alexander the Great.

Fluellen. Why, I pray you, is not pig great? the pig, or the great, or the mighty, or the huge, or the magnanimous, are all one reckonings, save the phrase is a little variations.   17

Gower. I think Alexander the Great was born in Macedon: his father was called Philip of Macedon, as I take it.

Fluellen. I think it is in Macedon where Alexander is porn. I tell you, captain, if you look in the maps of the world, I warrant you sall find, in the comparisons petween Macedon and Monmouth, that the situations, look you, is poth alike. There is a river in Macedon; and there is also moreover a river at Monmouth: it is called Wye at Monmouth; but it is out of my prains what is the name of the other river; but 't is all one, 't is alike as my fingers is to my fingers, and there is salmons in poth. If you mark Alexander's life well, Harry of Monmouth's life is come after it indifferent well; for there is figures in all things. Alexander, Got knows, and you know, in his rages, and his furies, and his wraths, and his cholers, and his moods, and his displeasures, and his indignations, and also peing a little intoxicates in his prains, did, in his ales and his angers, look you, kill his pest friend, Cleitus.   34

Gower. Our king is not like him in that: he never killed any of his friends.

Fluellen. It is not well done, mark you now, to take the tales out of my mouth, ere it is made and finished. I speak but in the figures and comparisons of it: as Alexander killed his friend Cleitus, peing in his ales and his cups, so also Harry Monmouth, peing in his right wits and his goot judgments, turned away the fat knight with the great pelly doublet: he was full of jests, and gipes, and knaveries, and mocks; I have forgot his name.   44

Gower. Sir John Falstaff.

Fluellen. That is he: I 'll tell you there is goot men porn at Monmouth.

Gower. Here comes his majesty.

Alarum.   Enter KING HENRY *and forces,* WARWICK, GLOU-
        CESTER, EXETER, *and others.*

   King Henry. I was not angry since I came to France
Until this instant.—Take a trumpet, herald;   50
Ride thou unto the horsemen on yon hill:
If they will fight with us, bid them come down,
Or void the field; they do offend our sight.
If they 'll do neither, we will come to them,
And make them skirr away as swift as stones
Enforced from the old Assyrian slings.
Besides, we 'll cut the throats of those we have,
And not a man of them that we shall take
Shall taste our mercy.   Go and tell them so.

Enter MONTJOY.

   Exeter. Here comes the herald of the French, my liege.
   Gloucester. His eyes are humbler than they us'd to
   be.   61
   King Henry. How now! what means this, herald? know'st
   thou not
That I have fin'd these bones of mine for ransom?
Com'st thou again for ransom?
   Montjoy.   No, great king:
I come to thee for charitable license,
That we may wander o'er this bloody field
To look our dead, and then to bury them;
To sort our nobles from our common men.
For many of our princes—woe the while!—
Lie drown'd and soak'd in mercenary blood;   70
So do our vulgar drench their peasant limbs
In blood of princes; and their wounded steeds
Fret fetlock deep in gore, and with wild rage
Yerk out their armed heels at their dead masters,
Killing them twice.   O, give us leave, great king,

To view the field in safety, and dispose
Of their dead bodies!

King Henry.　　　　I tell thee truly, herald,
I know not if the day be ours or no;
For yet a many of your horsemen peer
And gallop o'er the field.

Montjoy.　　　　The day is yours.　　80

King Henry. Praised be God, and not our strength, for it!
What is this castle call'd that stands hard by?

Montjoy. They call it Agincourt.

King Henry. Then call we this the field of Agincourt,
Fought on the day of Crispin Crispianus.

Fluellen. Your grandfather of famous memory, an 't please
your majesty, and your great-uncle Edward the Plack Prince
of Wales, as I have read in the chronicles, fought a most
prave pattle here in France.

King Henry. They did, Fluellen.　　90

Fluellen. Your majesty says very true: if your majesties is
remembered of it, the Welshmen did goot service in a garden where leeks did grow, wearing leeks in their Monmouth
caps; which, your majesty know, to this hour is an honourable padge of the service; and I do pelieve your majesty
takes no scorn to wear the leek upon Saint Tavy's day.

King Henry. I wear it for a memorable honour;
For I am Welsh, you know, good countryman.

Fluellen. All the water in Wye cannot wash your majesty's
Welsh ploot out of your pody, I can tell you that: Got pless
it and preserve it, as long as it pleases his grace, and his
majesty too!　　102

King Henry. Thanks, good my countryman.

Fluellen. By Cheshu, I am your majesty's countryman, I
care not who know it; I will confess it to all the world: I
need not to pe ashamed of your majesty, praised pe Got,
so long as your majesty is an honest man.

King Henry. God keep me so!—Our heralds go with him

Bring me just notice of the numbers dead
On both our parts.—Call yonder fellow hither.   110

       [*Points to Williams.   Exeunt Heralds with Montjoy.*

Exeter. Soldier, you must come to the king.

King Henry. Soldier, why wearest thou that glove in thy
    cap?

Williams. An 't please your majesty, 't is the gage of one
that I should fight withal, if he be alive.

King Henry. An Englishman?

Williams. An 't please your majesty, a rascal that swaggered with me last night; who, if alive and ever dare to
challenge this glove, I have sworn to take him a box o' th'
ear: or if I can see my glove in his cap, which he swore, as
he was a soldier, he would wear if alive, I will strike it
out soundly.   121

King Henry. What think you, Captain Fluellen? is it fit
this soldier keep his oath?

Fluellen. He is a craven and a villain else, an 't please
your majesty, in my conscience.

King Henry. It may be his enemy is a gentleman of great
sort, quite from the answer of his degree.

Fluellen. Though he pe as goot a gentleman as the tevil
is, as Lucifer and Pelzebub himself, it is necessary, look your
grace, that he keep his vow and his oath: if he pe perjured,
see you now, his reputation is as arrant a villain and a Jack-
sauce, as ever his plack shoe trod upon Got's ground and
his earth, in my conscience, la!   133

King Henry. Then keep thy vow, sirrah, when thou meet-
est the fellow.

Williams. So I will, my liege, as I live.

King Henry. Who servest thou under?

Williams. Under Captain Gower, my liege.

Fluellen. Gower is a goot captain, and is goot knowledge
and literatured in the wars.   140

King Henry. Call him hither to me, soldier.

Williams. I will, my liege.   [*Exit.*

King Henry. Here, Fluellen; wear thou this favour for
me and stick it in thy cap: when Alençon and myself were
down together, I plucked this glove from his helm: if any
man challenge this, he is a friend to Alençon, and an enemy
to our person; if thou encounter any such, apprehend him,
an thou dost me love.   148

Fluellen. Your grace does me as great honours as can pe
desired in the hearts of his subjects: I would fain see the
man, that has but two legs, that shall find himself aggriefed
at this glove, that is all; but I would fain see it once, an
please Got of his grace that I might see.

King Henry. Knowest thou Gower?

Fluellen. He is my dear friend, an please you.

King Henry. Pray thee, go seek him, and bring him to
my tent.

Fluellen. I will fetch him.   [*Exit.*

King Henry. My Lord of Warwick, and my brother Glou-
　　　cester,
Follow Fluellen closely at the heels: 160
The glove which I have given him for a favour
May haply purchase him a box o' th' ear;
It is the soldier's: I by bargain should
Wear it myself.   Follow, good cousin Warwick:
If that the soldier strike him, as I judge
By his blunt bearing he will keep his word,
Some sudden mischief may arise of it;
For I do know Fluellen valiant
And, touch'd with choler, hot as gunpowder,
And quickly will return an injury: 170
Follow, and see there be no harm between them.—
Go you with me, uncle of Exeter.   [*Exeunt.*

SCENE VIII. *Before King Henry's Pavilion.*

Enter GOWER *and* WILLIAMS.

Williams. I warrant it is to knight you, captain.

Enter FLUELLEN.

Fluellen. Got's will and his pleasure, captain, I peseech
you now, come apace to the king: there is more goot toward
you peradventure than is in your knowledge to dream of.

Williams. Sir, know you this glove?

Fluellen. Know the glove! I know the glove is a glove.

Williams. I know this, and thus I challenge it.

[*Strikes him.*

Fluellen. 'Sblood! an arrant traitor as any is in the universal world, or in France, or in England!

Gower. How now, sir! you villain!

Williams. Do you think I'll be forsworn?   10

Fluellen. Stand away, Captain Gower; I will give treason
his payment into plows, I warrant you.

Williams. I am no traitor.

Fluellen. That's a lie in thy throat.—I charge you in his
majesty's name, apprehend him: he's a friend of the Duke
Alençon's.

Enter WARWICK *and* GLOUCESTER.

Warwick. How now, how now! what's the matter?

Fluellen. My Lord of Warwick, here is—praised pe Got
for it!—a most contagious treason come to light, look
you, as you shall desire in a summer's day. Here is his
majesty.

Enter KING HENRY *and* EXETER.

King Henry. How now! what's the matter?   22

Fluellen. My liege, here is a villain and a traitor, that, look

your grace, has struck the glove which your majesty is take
out of the helmet of Alençon.

Williams. My liege, this was my glove; here is the fellow
of it; and he that I gave it to in change promised to wear it
in his cap: I promised to strike him, if he did. I met this
man with my glove in his cap, and I have been as good as
my word.   30

Fluellen. Your majesty hear now, saving your majesty's
manhood, what an arrant, rascally, peggarly, lousy knave it
is: I hope your majesty is pear me testimony and witness,
and will avouchment, that this is the glove of Alençon, that
your majesty is give me; in your conscience, now?

King Henry. Give me thy glove, soldier: look, here is the
fellow of it.
'T was I, indeed, thou promised'st to strike;
And thou hast given me most bitter terms.

Fluellen. An please your majesty, let his neck answer for
it, if there is any martial law in the world.   41

King Henry. How canst thou make me satisfaction?

Williams. All offences, my lord, come from the heart:
never came any from mine that might offend your majesty.

King Henry. It was ourself thou didst abuse.

Williams. Your majesty came not like yourself: you appeared to me but as a common man; witness the night, your
garments, your lowliness; and what your highness suffered
under that shape, I beseech you take it for your own fault
and not mine: for had you been as I took you for, I made
no offence; therefore, I beseech your highness, pardon me.

King Henry. Here, uncle Exeter, fill this glove with
    crowns,   52
And give it to this fellow.—Keep it, fellow;
And wear it for an honour in thy cap
Till I do challenge it.—Give him the crowns:
And, captain, you must needs be friends with him.

Fluellen. Py this day and this light, the fellow has mettle

enough in his pelly. Hold, there is twelve pence for you,
and I pray you to serve Got, and keep you out of prawls,
and prabbles, and quarrels, and dissensions, and, I warrant
you, it is the petter for you.   63

Williams. I will none of your money.

Fluellen. It is with a goot will; I can tell you, it will serve
you to mend your shoes: come, wherefore should you pe so
pashful? your shoes is not so goot: 't is a goot silling, I
warrant you, or I will change it.

Enter an English Herald.

King Henry. Now, herald, are the dead number'd?

Herald. Here is the number of the slaughter'd French.

King Henry. What prisoners of good sort are taken,
        uncle?   71

Exeter. Charles Duke of Orleans, nephew to the king;
John Duke of Bourbon, and Lord Bouciqualt:
Of other lords and barons, knights and squires,
Full fifteen hundred, besides common men.

King Henry. This note doth tell me of ten thousand
        French
That in the field lie slain: of princes, in this number,
And nobles bearing banners, there lie dead
One hundred twenty-six: added to these,
Of knights, esquires, and gallant gentlemen,   80
Eight thousand and four hundred; of the which,
Five hundred were but yesterday dubb'd knights:
So that, in these ten thousand they have lost,
There are but sixteen hundred mercenaries;
The rest are princes, barons, lords, knights, squires,
And gentlemen of blood and quality.
The names of those their nobles that lie dead:
Charles Delabreth, high constable of France;
Jacques of Chatillon, admiral of France;
The master of the cross-bows, Lord Rambures;   90

Great Master of France, the brave Sir Guichard Dauphin,
John Duke of Alençon, Anthony Duke of Brabant,
The brother to the Duke of Burgundy,
And Edward Duke of Bar: of lusty earls,
Grandpré and Roussi, Fauconberg and Foix,
Beaumont and Marle, Vaudemont and Lestrale.
Here was a royal fellowship of death!—
Where is the number of our English dead?

> *[Herald shows him another paper*

Edward the Duke of York, the Earl of Suffolk,
Sir Richard Ketly, Davy Gam, esquire: 100
None else of name; and of all other men
But five and twenty.—O God, thy arm was here;
And not to us, but to thy arm alone,
Ascribe we all!—When, without stratagem,
But in plain shock and even play of battle,
Was ever known so great and little loss
On one part and on the other?—Take it, God,
For it is none but thine!

 Exeter.   'T is wonderful!

 King Henry. Come, go we in procession to the village:
And be it death proclaimed through our host   110
To boast of this, or take that praise from God
Which is his only.

 Fluellen. Is it not lawful, an please your majesty, to tell
how many is killed?

 King Henry. Yes, captain; but with this acknowledgment,
That God fought for us.

 Fluellen. Yes, my conscience, he did us great goot.

 King Henry. Do we all holy rites;
Let there be sung 'Non nobis' and 'Te Deum.'
The dead with charity enclos'd in clay,   120
We'll then to Calais; and to England then;
Where ne'er from France arriv'd more happy men. *[Exeunt.*

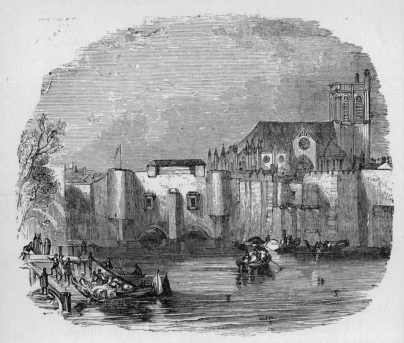

TROYES.

ACT V.

PROLOGUE.

Enter Chorus.

Chorus. Vouchsafe to those that have not read the story,
That I may prompt them: and of such as have,
I humbly pray them to admit the excuse
Of time, of numbers, and due course of things,
Which cannot in their huge and proper life
Be here presented.   Now we bear the king

Toward Calais: grant him there; there seen,
Heave him away upon your winged thoughts
Athwart the sea.   Behold, the English beach
Pales in the flood with men, with wives, and boys,   16
Whose shouts and claps out-voice the deep-mouth'd sea,
Which like a mighty whiffler fore the king
Seems to prepare his way: so let him land,
And solemnly see him set on to London.
So swift a pace hath thought that even now
You may imagine him upon Blackheath;
Where that his lords desire him to have borne
His bruised helmet and his bended sword
Before him through the city: he forbids it,
Being free from vainness and self-glorious pride;   20
Giving full trophy, signal, and ostent
Quite from himself to God.   But now behold,
In the quick forge and working-house of thought,
How London doth pour out her citizens!
The mayor and all his brethren in best sort,
Like to the senators of the antique Rome,
With the plebeians swarming at their heels,
Go forth and fetch their conquering Cæsar in;
As, by a lower but loving likelihood,
Were now the general of our gracious empress,   30
As in good time he may, from Ireland coming,
Bringing rebellion broached on his sword,
How many would the peaceful city quit,
To welcome him! much more, and much more cause,
Did they this Harry.   Now in London place him;—
As yet the lamentation of the French
Invites the King of England's stay at home;
The emperor coming in behalf of France,
To order peace between them;—and omit
All the occurrences, whatever chanc'd,   40
Till Harry's back-return again to France:

There must we bring him; and myself have play'd
The interim, by remembering you 't is past.
Then brook abridgment, and your eyes advance,
After your thoughts, straight back again to France.   [*Exit.*

Scene I. *France. The English Camp.*
Enter Fluellen *and* Gower.

Gower. Nay, that 's right; but why wear you your leek
to-day? Saint Davy's day is past.

Fluellen. There is occasions and causes why and wherefore in all things: I will tell you, as my friend, Captain
Gower: the rascally, scald, peggarly, lousy, pragging knave,
Pistol, which you and yourself and all the world know to pe
no petter than a fellow, look you now, of no merits, he is
come to me and prings me pread and salt yesterday, look
you, and pid me eat my leek: it was in a place where I could
not preed no contention with him; but I will pe so pold as
to wear it in my cap till I see him once again, and then I
will tell him a little piece of my desires.   12

Enter Pistol.

Gower. Why, here he comes, swelling like a turkey-cock.

Fluellen. 'T is no matter for his swellings nor his turkey-
cocks.—Got pless you, Aunchient Pistol! you scurvy, lousy
knave, Got pless you!

Pistol. Ha! art thou bedlam? dost thou thirst, base Trojan,
To have me fold up Parca's fatal web?
Hence! I am qualmish at the smell of leek.

Fluellen. I peseech you heartily, scurvy, lousy knave, at my
desires, and my requests, and my petitions, to eat, look you,
this leek: because, look you, you do not love it, nor your
affections and your appetites and your digestions does not
agree with it, I would desire you to eat it.   24

Pistol. Not for Cadwallader and all his goats.

Fluellen. There is one goat for you. [*Strikes him.*] Will you pe so goot, scald knave, as eat it?

Pistol. Base Trojan, thou shalt die.

Fluellen. You say very true, scald knave, when Got's will is: I will desire you to live in the mean time, and eat your victuals: come, there is sauce for it. [*Strikes him.*] You called me yesterday mountain-squire; but I will make you to-day a squire of low degree. I pray you, fall to: if you can mock a leek, you can eat a leek.   34

Gower. Enough, captain: you have astonished him.

Fluellen. I say, I will make him eat some part of my leek, or I will peat his pate four days.—Pite, I pray you; it is goot for your green wound and your ploody coxcomb.

Pistol. Must I bite?

Fluellen. Yes, certainly, and out of doubt and out of question too, and ambiguities.   41

Pistol. By this leek, I will most horribly revenge: I eat, and yet I swear—

Fluellen. Eat, I pray you: will you have some more sauce to your leek? there is not enough leek to swear py.

Pistol. Quiet thy cudgel; thou dost see I eat.

Fluellen. Much goot do you, scald knave, heartily. Nay, pray you, throw none away; the skin is goot for your proken coxcomb. When you take occasions to see leeks hereafter, I pray you, mock at 'em; that is all.   50

Pistol. Good.

Fluellen. Ay, leeks is goot. Hold you, there is a groat to heal your pate.

Pistol. Me a groat!

Fluellen. Yes, verily and in truth, you shall take it, or I have another leek in my pocket, which you shall eat.

Pistol. I take thy groat in earnest of revenge.

Fluellen. If I owe you any thing, I will pay you in cudgels: you shall pe a woodmonger, and puy nothing of me but cudgels. Got b' wi' you, and keep you, and heal your pate.   60

[*Exit.*

Pistol. All hell shall stir for this.

Gower. Go, go; you are a counterfeit cowardly knave.
Will you mock at an ancient tradition, begun upon an honourable respect, and worn as a memorable trophy of prede-
ceased valour, and dare not avouch in your deeds any of your
words? I have seen you gleeking and galling at this gentleman twice or thrice. You thought, because he could not
speak English in the native garb, he could not therefore
handle an English cudgel: you find it otherwise; and hence-
forth let a Welsh correction teach you a good English condition. Fare ye well. [*Exit.*

Pistol. Doth Fortune play the huswife with me now? 　72
News have I, that my Nell is dead i' the spital
Of malady of France;
And there my rendezvous is quite cut off.
Old I do wax; and from my weary limbs
Honour is cudgell'd. Well, bawd will I turn,
And something lean to cutpurse of quick hand.
To England will I steal, and there I' ll steal:
And patches will I get unto these cudgell'd scars,
And swear I got them in the Gallia wars. [*Exit.*

SCENE II. *Troyes. A Room in the Palace.*

Enter, at one door, KING HENRY, EXETER, BEDFORD, GLOU-
CESTER, WARWICK, WESTMORELAND, *and other* Lords; *at
another, the* FRENCH KING, QUEEN ISABEL, *the* PRINCESS
KATHERINE, ALICE, *and other* Ladies, *the* DUKE OF BUR-
GUNDY, *and his train.*

King Henry. Peace to this meeting, wherefore we are met!
Unto our brother France, and to our sister,
Health and fair time of day; joy and good wishes
To our most fair and princely cousin Katherine;
And, as a branch and member of this royalty,
By whom this great assembly is contriv'd,

We do salute you, Duke of Burgundy;
And, princes French, and peers, health to you all!

 French King. Right joyous are we to behold your face,
Most worthy brother England; fairly met: 10
So are you, princes English, every one.

 Queen Isabel. So happy be the issue, brother England,
Of this good day and of this gracious meeting,
As we are now glad to behold your eyes;
Your eyes, which hitherto have borne in them
Against the French, that met them in their bent,
The fatal balls of murthering basilisks:
The venom of such looks, we fairly hope,
Have lost their quality, and that this day
Shall change all griefs and quarrels into love. 20

 King Henry. To cry amen to that, thus we appear.

 Queen Isabel. You English princes all, I do salute you.

 Burgundy. My duty to you both, on equal love,
Great Kings of France and England! That I have labour'd
With all my wits, my pains, and strong endeavours,
To bring your most imperial majesties
Unto this bar and royal interview,
Your mightiness on both parts best can witness.
Since then my office hath so far prevail'd
That, face to face and royal eye to eye,   30
You have congreeted, let it not disgrace me,
If I demand, before this royal view,
What rub or what impediment there is,
Why that the naked, poor, and mangled Peace,
Dear nurse of arts, plenties, and joyful births,
Should not in this best garden of the world,
Our fertile France, put up her lovely visage?
Alas, she hath from France too long been chas'd,
And all her husbandry doth lie on heaps,
Corrupting in it own fertility.   40
Her vine, the merry cheerer of the heart,

Unpruned dies; her hedges even-pleach'd,
Like prisoners wildly overgrown with hair,
Put forth disorder'd twigs; her fallow leas
The darnel, hemlock, and rank fumitory
Doth root upon, while that the coulter rusts
That should deracinate such savagery:
The even mead, that erst brought sweetly forth
The freckled cowslip, burnet, and green clover,
Wanting the scythe, all uncorrected, rank,   50
Conceives by idleness, and nothing teems
But hateful docks, rough thistles, kecksies, burs,
Losing both beauty and utility.
And as our vineyards, fallows, meads, and hedges,
Defective in their natures, grow to wildness,
Even so our houses and ourselves and children
Have lost, or do not learn for want of time,
The sciences that should become our country;
But grow like savages,—as soldiers will
That nothing do but meditate on blood,—   60
To swearing and stern looks, diffus'd attire,
And every thing that seems unnatural.
Which to reduce into our former favour
You are assembled: and my speech entreats
That I may know the let, why gentle Peace
Should not expel these inconveniences
And bless us with her former qualities.

King Henry. If, Duke of Burgundy, you would the peace,
Whose want gives growth to the imperfections
Which you have cited, you must buy that peace   70
With full accord to all our just demands;
Whose tenours and particular effects
You have enschedul'd briefly in your hands.

Burgundy. The king hath heard them; to the which
  as yet
There is no answer made.

King Henry.   Well then the peace,
Which you before so urg'd, lies in his answer.
   French King. I have but with a cursorary eye
O'erglanc'd the articles : pleaseth your grace
To appoint some of your council presently
To sit with us once more, with better heed   80
To re-survey them, we will suddenly
Pass our accept and peremptory answer.
   King Henry. Brother, we shall.—Go, uncle Exeter,
And brother Clarence, and you, brother Gloucester,
Warwick and Huntingdon, go with the king ;
And take with you free power to ratify,
Augment, or alter, as your wisdoms best
Shall see advantageable for our dignity,
Any thing in or out of our demands,
And we 'll consign thereto.—Will you, fair sister,   90
Go with the princes, or stay here with us ?
   Queen Isabel. Our gracious brother, I will go with them :
Haply a woman's voice may do some good,
When articles too nicely urg'd be stood on.
   King Henry. Yet leave our cousin Katherine here with us
She is our capital demand, compris'd
Within the fore-rank of our articles.
   Queen Isabel. She hath good leave.
      [*Exeunt all except Henry, Katherine, and Alice.*
   King Henry.   Fair Katherine, and most fair,
Will you vouchsafe to teach a soldier terms
Such as will enter at a lady's ear   100
And plead his love-suit to her gentle heart ?
   Katherine. Your majesty sall mock at me ; I cannot speak
your England.
   King Henry. O fair Katherine, if you will love me soundly
with your French heart, I will be glad to hear you confess it
brokenly with your English tongue. Do you like me, Kate ?
   Katherine. Pardonnez-moi, I cannot tell vat is 'like me.'

King Henry. An angel is like you, Kate, and you are like an angel.

Katherine. Que dit-il? que je suis semblable à les anges?

Alice. Oui, vraiment, sauf votre grace, ainsi dit-il.   111

King Henry. I said so, dear Katherine; and I must not blush to affirm it.

Katherine. O bon Dieu! les langues des hommes sont pleines de tromperies.

King Henry. What says she, fair one? that the tongues of men are full of deceits?

Alice. Oui, dat de tongues of de mans is be full of deceits: dat is de princess.

King Henry. The princess is the better Englishwoman. I' faith, Kate, my wooing is fit for thy understanding: I am glad thou canst speak no better English; for, if thou couldst, thou wouldst find me such a plain king that thou wouldst think I had sold my farm to buy my crown. I know no ways to mince it in love, but directly to say 'I love you:' then if you urge me farther than to say 'do you in faith?' I wear out my suit. Give me your answer; i' faith, do: and so clap hands and a bargain: how say you, lady?   128

Katherine. Sauf votre honneur, me understand vell.

King Henry. Marry, if you would put me to verses or to dance for your sake, Kate, why you undid me: for the one, I have neither words nor measure; and for the other, I have no strength in measure, yet a reasonable measure in strength. If I could win a lady at leap-frog, or by vaulting into my saddle with my armour on my back, under the correction of bragging be it spoken, I should quickly leap into a wife. Or if I might buffet for my love, or bound my horse for her favours, I could lay on like a butcher and sit like a jack-an-apes, never off. But, before God, Kate, I cannot look green-ly nor gasp out my eloquence, nor I have no cunning in prot-estation; only downright oaths, which I never use till urged, nor never break for urging. If thou canst love a fellow of this temper, Kate, whose face is not worth sun-burning, that never looks in his glass for love of any thing he sees there, let thine eye be thy cook. I speak to thee plain soldier: if thou canst love me for this, take me; if not, to say to thee that I shall die, is true; but for thy love, by the Lord, no; yet I love thee too. And while thou livest, dear Kate, take a fellow of plain and uncoined constancy; for he perforce must do thee right, because he hath not the gift to woo in other places: for these fellows of infinite tongue, that can rhyme themselves into ladies' favours, they do always reason themselves out again. What! a speaker is but a prater; a rhyme is but a ballad. A good leg will fall; a straight back will stoop; a black beard will turn white; a curled pate will grow bald; a fair face will wither; a full eye will wax hollow: but a good heart, Kate, is the sun and the moon; or rather the sun and not the moon; for it shines bright and never changes, but keeps his course truly. If thou would have such a one, take me; and take me, take a soldier; take a soldier, take a king. And what sayest thou then to my love? speak, my fair, and fairly, I pray thee. 162

Katherine. Is it possible dat I sould love de enemy of France?

King Henry. No; it is not possible you should love the enemy of France, Kate: but, in loving me, you should love the friend of France; for I love France so well that I will not part with a village of it; I will have it all mine: and, Kate, when France is mine and I am yours, then yours is France and you are mine. 170

Katherine. I cannot tell vat is dat.

King Henry. No, Kate? I will tell thee in French; which I am sure will hang upon my tongue like a new-married wife about her husband's neck, hardly to be shook off. Quand j'ai le possession de France, et quand vous avez le possession de moi,—let me see, what then? Saint Denis be my speed!—donc votre est France et vous êtes mienne. It is

as easy for me, Kate, to conquer the kingdom as to speak
so much more French: I shall never move thee in French,
unless it be to laugh at me.   180

Katherine. Sauf votre honneur, le Français que vous
parlez, il est meilleur que l'Anglais lequel je parle.

King Henry. No, faith, is 't not, Kate: but thy speaking
of my tongue, and I thine, most truly-falsely, must needs be
granted to be much at one. But, Kate, dost thou understand thus much English, canst thou love me?

Katherine. I cannot tell.

King Henry. Can any of your neighbours tell, Kate? I 'll
ask them. Come, I know thou lovest me: and at night,
when you come into your closet, you 'll question this gentlewoman about me; and I know, Kate, you will to her dis-
praise those parts in me that you love with your heart: but,
good Kate, mock me mercifully; the rather, gentle princess,
because I love thee cruelly. If ever thou beest mine, Kate,
as I have a saving faith within me tells me thou shalt, I get
thee with scambling, and thou must therefore needs prove
a good soldier-breeder. What sayest thou, my fair flower-
de-luce?

Katherine. I do not know dat.   199

King Henry. No; 't is hereafter to know, but now to
promise: do but now promise, Kate, you will endeavour
for your French part, and for my English moiety take the
word of a king and a bachelor. How answer you, la plus
belle Katherine du monde, mon très-cher et divin déesse?

Katherine. Your majestee ave fausse French enough to
deceive de most sage demoiselle dat is en France.

King Henry. Now, fie upon my false French! By mine
honour, in true English, I love thee, Kate: by which honour
I dare not swear thou lovest me; yet my blood begins to
flatter me that thou dost, notwithstanding the poor and untempering effect of my visage. Now, beshrew my father's
ambition! he was thinking of civil wars when he got me:

therefore was I created with a stubborn outside, with an aspect of iron, that, when I come to woo ladies, I fright them. But, in faith, Kate, the elder I wax, the better I shall appear: my comfort is, that old age, that ill layer up of beauty, can do no more spoil upon my face: thou hast me, if thou hast me, at the worst; and thou shalt wear me, if thou wear me, better and better: and therefore tell me, most fair Katherine, will you have me? Put off your maiden blushes; avouch the thoughts of your heart with the looks of an empress; take me by the hand, and say 'Harry of England, I am thine :' which word thou shalt no sooner bless mine ear withal, but I will tell thee aloud 'England is thine, Ireland is thine, France is thine, and Henry Plantagenet is thine ;' who, though I speak it before his face, if he be not fellow with the best king, thou shalt find the best king of good fellows. Come, your answer in broken music; for thy voice is music and thy English broken; therefore, queen of all, Katherine, break thy mind to me in broken English; wilt thou have me? 231

Katherine. Dat is as it sall please de roi mon père.

King Henry. Nay, it will please him well, Kate; it shall please him, Kate.

Katherine. Den it sall also content me.

King Henry. Upon that I kiss your hand, and I call you my queen.

Katherine. Laissez, mon seigneur, laissez, laissez: ma foi, je ne veux point que vous abaissiez votre grandeur en baisant la main d'une votre indigne serviteur; excusez-moi, je vous supplie, mon très-puissant seigneur. 241

King Henry. Then I will kiss your lips, Kate.

Katherine. Les dames et demoiselles pour être baisées devant leur noces, il n'est pas la coûtume de France.

King Henry. Madam my interpreter, what says she?

Alice. Dat it is not be de fashion pour les ladies of France,—I cannot tell vat is baiser en Anglish.

King Henry. To kiss.

Alice. Your majesty entendre bettre que moi.

King Henry. It is not a fashion for the maids in France to kiss before they are married, would she say?   251

Alice. Oui, vraiment.

King Henry. O Kate, nice customs curtsy to great kings. Dear Kate, you and I cannot be confined within the weak list of a country's fashion : we are the makers of manners, Kate; and the liberty that follows our places stops the mouth of all find-faults; as I will do yours, for upholding the nice fashion of your country in denying me a kiss: therefore, patiently and yielding. [*Kissing her.*] You have witchcraft in your lips, Kate : there is more eloquence in a sugar touch of them than in the tongues of the French council; and they should sooner persuade Harry of England than a general petition of monarchs.   Here comes your father.   263

Re-enter the FRENCH KING *and his* QUEEN, BURGUNDY, *and other* Lords.

Burgundy. God save your majesty! my royal cousin, teach you our princess English?

King Henry. I would have her learn, my fair cousin, how perfectly I love her; and that is good English.

Burgundy. Is she not apt?

King Henry. Our tongue is rough, coz, and my condition is not smooth; so that, having neither the voice nor the heart of flattery about me, I cannot so conjure up the spirit of love in her, that he will appear in his true likeness.   272

Burgundy. Pardon the frankness of my mirth, if I answer you for that.   If you would conjure in her, you must make a circle; if conjure up love in her in his true likeness, he must appear naked and blind.   Can you blame her then, being a maid yet rosed over with the virgin crimson of modesty, if she deny the appearance of a naked blind boy? It were, my lord, a hard condition for a maid to consign to

King Henry. Yet they do wink and yield, as love is blind
and enforces.   281

Burgundy. They are then excused, my lord, when they
see not what they do.

King Henry. Then, good my lord, teach your cousin to
consent winking.

Burgundy. I will wink on her to consent, my lord, if you
will teach her to know my meaning: for maids, well sum-
mered and warm kept, are like flies at Bartholomew-tide,
blind, though they have their eyes.

King Henry. This moral ties me over to time and a hot
summer; and so I shall catch the fly, your cousin, in the
latter end, and she must be blind too.   292

Burgundy. As love is, my lord, before it loves.

King Henry. It is so: and you may, some of you, thank
love for my blindness, who cannot see many a fair French
city for one fair French maid that stands in my way.

French King. Yes, my lord, you see them perspectively,
the cities turned into a maid; for they are all girdled with
maiden walls that war hath never entered.

King Henry. Shall Kate be my wife?   300

French King. So please you.

King Henry. I am content; so the maiden cities you talk
of may wait on her: so the maid that stood in the way for
my wish shall show me the way to my will.

French King. We have consented to all terms of reason.

King Henry. Is 't so, my lords of England?

Westmoreland. The king hath granted every article:
His daughter first, and then in sequel all,
According to their firm proposed natures.

Exeter. Only he hath not yet subscribed this: 310
where your majesty demands that the King of France,
having any occasion to write for matter of grant, shall
name your highness in this form and with this addition, in
French, Notre très-cher fils Henri, roi d'Angleterre, héritier

de France ; and thus in Latin, Præclarissimus filius noster
Henricus, rex Angliæ, et hæres Franciæ.

French King. Nor this I have not, brother, so denied,
But your request shall make me let it pass.

King Henry. I pray you then, in love and dear alliance,
Let that one article rank with the rest;   32°
And thereupon give me your daughter.

French King. Take her, fair son, and from her blood
    raise up
Issue to me ; that the contending kingdoms
Of France and England, whose very shores look pale
With envy of each other's happiness,
May cease their hatred, and this dear conjunction
Plant neighbourhood and Christian-like accord
In their sweet bosoms, that never war advance
His bleeding sword 'twixt England and fair France.

All. Amen !   33°

King Henry. Now, welcome, Kate :—and bear me wit-
    ness all,
That here I kiss her as my sovereign queen.   [*Flourish.*

Queen Isabel. God, the best maker of all marriages,
Combine your hearts in one, your realms in one !
As man and wife, being two, are one in love,
So be there 'twixt your kingdoms such a spousal,
That never may ill office, or fell jealousy,
Which troubles oft the bed of blessed marriage,
Thrust in between the paction of these kingdoms,
To make divorce of their incorporate league ;   34°
That English may as French, French Englishmen,
Receive each other.   God speak this Amen !

All. Amen !

King Henry. Prepare we for our marriage :—on which
    day
My lord of Burgundy, we 'll take your oath,
And all the peers', for surety of our leagues.

Then shall I swear to Kate, and you to me;
And may our oaths well kept and prosperous be!

[Sennet. Exeunt

EPILOGUE.

Enter Chorus.

Chorus. Thus far, with rough and all-unable pen,
   Our bending author hath pursued the story,
In little room confining mighty men,
   Mangling by starts the full course of their glory.
Small time, but in that small most greatly liv'd
   This star of England: Fortune made his sword;
By which the world's best garden he achiev'd,
   And of it left his son imperial lord.
Henry the Sixth, in infant bands crown'd King
   Of France and England, did this king succeed;   10
Whose state so many had the managing,
   That they lost France and made his England bleed
Which oft our stage hath shown; and, for their sake,
In your fair minds let this acceptance take.

[Exit.

Pistol. By this leek, I will most **horribly revenge**: I eat, and yet I swear—(v. 1. 42).

NOTES.

ABBREVIATIONS USED IN THE NOTES.

Abbott (or Gr.), Abbott's *Shakespearian Grammar* (third edition).
A. S., Anglo-Saxon.
A. V., Authorized Version of the Bible (1611).
B. and F., Beaumont and Fletcher.
B. J., Ben Jonson.
Camb. ed., "Cambridge edition" of *Shakespeare*, edited by Clark and Wright.
Cf. (*confer*), compare.
Coll., Collier.
Coll. MS., Manuscript Corrections of Second Folio, edited by Collier.
D., Dyce.
H., Hudson.
Hen. VIII. (followed by reference to *page*), Rolfe's edition of *Henry VIII.*
Id. (*idem*), the same.
J. C. (followed by reference to *page*), Rolfe's edition of *Julius Cæsar.*
J. H., John Hunter's edition of *Henry V.* (London, n. d.).
K., Knight.
Macb. (followed by reference to *page*), Rolfe's edition of *Macbeth.*
Mer., Rolfe's edition of *The Merchant of Venice.*
M. N. D. (followed by reference to *page*), Rolfe's edition of *A Midsummer-Night's Dream.*
Nares, *Glossary*, edited by Halliwell and Wright (London, 1859).
Prol., Prologue.
Rich. II. (followed by reference to *page*), Rolfe's edition of *Richard II.*
S., Shakespeare.
Schmidt, A. Schmidt's *Shakespeare-Lexicon* (Berlin, 1874).
Sr., Singer.
St., Staunton.
Temp. (followed by reference to *page*), Rolfe's edition of *The Tempest.*
Theo., Theobald.
V., Verplanck.
W., White.
Walker, Wm. Sidney Walker's *Critical Examination of the Text of Shakespeare* (London, 1860).
Warb., Warburton.
Wb., Webster's Dictionary (revised quarto edition of 1864).
Worc., Worcester's Dictionary (quarto edition).

The abbreviations of the names of Shakespeare's Plays will be readily understood; as *T. N.* for *Twelfth Night, Cor.* for *Coriolanus,* 3 *Hen. VI.* for *The Third Part of King Henry the Sixth,* etc. *P. P.* refers to *The Passionate Pilgrim; V. and A.* to *Venus and Adonis; L. C.* to *Lover's Complaint;* and *Sonn.* to the *Sonnets.*

NOTES.

THE GLOBE THEATRE.

INTRODUCTION.

The following extracts from Holinshed (which we select from Halliwell's Introduction) contain the more important passages used by the poet in the play:—

A.D. 1413.—" Whilest in the Lent season the king laie at Killingworth, there came to him from Charles Dolphin of France certeine ambassadors, that brought with them a barrell of Paris balles, which from their maister they presented to him for a token that was taken in verie ill part, as sent in scorne, to signifie that it was more meet for the king to passe the time with such childish exercise, than to attempt any worthie exploit. Wherfore the K. wrote to him that, yer ought long, he would tosse him some London balles that perchance should shake the walles of the best court in France."

A.D. 1414.—" In the second yeare of his reigne, king Henrie called his
high court of parlement, the last daie of Aprill, in the towne of Leicester, in which parlement manie profitable lawes were concluded, and manie
petitions mooved, were for that time deferred.   Amongst which, one was,
that a bill exhibited in the parlement holden at Westminster in the eleventh yeare of king Henrie the fourth (which, by reason the king was
then troubled with civill discord, came to none effect) might now with
good deliberation be pondered, and brought to some good conclusion.
The effect of which supplication was, that the temporall lands devoutlie
given, and disordinatelie spent by religious, and other spirituall persons,
should be seized into the kings hands, sith the same might suffice to
mainteine, to the honor of the king, and defense of the realme, fifteene
earls, fifteene hundred knights, six thousand and two hundred esquiers,
and a hundred almesse-houses, for reliefe onlie of the poore, impotent,
and needie persons, and the king to have cleerlie to his coffers twentie
thousand pounds, with manie other provisions and values of religious
houses, which I passe over.

" This bill was much noted, and more feared among the religious
sort, whom suerlie it touched verie neere, and therefore to find remedie
against it, they determined to assaie all waies to put by and overthrow
this bill ; wherein they thought best to trie if they might moove the
kings mood with some sharpe invention, that he should not regard the
importunate petitions of the commons.   Whereupon, on a daie in the
parlement, Henrie Chichelie, archbishop of Canturburie, made a pithie
oration, wherein he declared, how not onelie the duchies of Normandie
and Aquitaine, with the counties of Anjou and Maine, and the countrie
of Gascoigne, were by undoubted title apperteining to the king, as to the
lawfull and onelie heire of the same ; but also to the whole realme of
France, as heire to his great grandfather king Edward the third.

" Herein did he much inveie against the surmised and false fained law
Salike which the Frenchmen alledge ever against the kings of England
in barre of their just title to the crowne of France.   The verie words of
that supposed law are these, *In terram Salicam mulieres ne succedant*,
that is to saie, into the Salike land let not women succeed.   Which the
French glossers expound to be the realme of France, and that this law
was made by king Pharamond ; whereas yet their owne authors affirme
that the land Salike is in Germanie betweene the rivers of Elbe and
Sala ; and that when Charles the great had overcome the Saxons, he
placed there certeine Frenchmen, which having in disdeine the dishonest
maners of the Germane women, made a law, that the females should not
succeed to any inheritance within that land, which at this daie is called
Meisen, so that, if this be true, this law was not made for the realme of
France, nor the Frenchmen possessed the land Salike, till foure hundred
and one and twentie yeares after the death of Pharamond, the supposed
maker of this Salike law, for this Pharamond deceased in the yeare 426,
and Charles the great subdued the Saxons, and placed the Frenchmen
in those parts beyond the river of Sala, in the yeare 805.

" Moreover, it appeareth by their owne writers that king Pepine, which
deposed Childerike, claimed the crowne of France, as heire generall, for

that he was descended of Blithild, daughter to king Clothair the first : Hugh Capet also, who usurped the crowne upon Charles Duke of Loraine, the sole heire male of the line and stocke of Charles the great, to make his title seeme true, and appeare good, though in deed it was starke naught, conveied himselfe as heire to the ladie Lingard, daughter to king Charlemaine sonne to Lewes the emperour, that was son to Charles the great. King Lewes also the tenth, otherwise called saint Lewes, being verie heir to the said usurper Hugh Capet, could never be satisfied in his conscience how he might justlie keepe and possesse the crowne of France, till he was persuaded and fullie instructed that queene Isabell his grandmother was lineallie descended of the ladie Ermengard daughter and heire to the above named Charles duke of Loraine, by the which marriage, the bloud and line of Charles the great was againe united and restored to the crowne and scepter of France, so that more cleeare than the sunne it openlie appeareth that the title of king Pepin, the claime of Hugh Capet, the possession of Lewes, yea and the French kings to this daie, are derived and conveied from the heire female, though they would under the colour of such a fained law, barre the kings and princes of this realme of England of their right and lawfull inheritance.

" The archbishop further alledged out of the booke of Numbers this saieing : ' When a man dieth without a sonne, let the inheritance descend to his daughter.' At length, having said sufficientlie for the proofe of the kings just and lawfull title to the crowne of France, he exhorted him to advance foorth his banner to fight for his right, to conquer his inheritance, to spare neither bloud, sword, nor fire, sith his warre was just, his cause good, and his claime true. And to the intent his loving chapleins and obedient subjects of the spiritualtie might show themselves willing and desirous to aid his majestie, for the recoverie of his ancient right and true inheritance, the archbishop declared that in their spirituall convocation, they had granted to his highnesse such a summe of monie, as never by no spirituall persons was to any prince before those daies given or advanced.

" When the archbishop had ended his prepared tale, Rafe Nevill, earle of Westmerland, and as then lord Warden of the marches against Scotland, understanding that the king, upon a couragious desire to recover his right in France, would suerlie take the wars in hand, thought good to moove the king to begin first with Scotland, and thereupon declared how easie a matter it should be to make a conquest there, and how greatlie the same should further his wished purpose for the subduing of the Frenchmen, concluding the sum of his tale with this old saying : that *Who so will France win, must with Scotland first begin.* Many matters he touched, as well to show how necessarie the conquest of Scotland should be, as also to proove how just a cause the king had to attempt it ; trusting to persuade the king and all other to be of his opinion.

" But after he had made an end, the duke of Excester, uncle to the king, a man well learned and wise, who had beene sent into Italie by his father, intending that he should have been a preest, replied against the erle of Westmerlands oration, affirming rather that he which would Scotland win, he with France must first begin. For if the king might once compasse the conquest of France, Scotland could not long resist; so that conquere France, and Scotland would soon obeie. For where should the Scots lerne policie and skill to defend themselves if they had not their bringing up and training in France. If the French pensions maintained not the Scottish nobilitie, in what case should they be. Then take awaie France, and the Scots will soon be tamed; France being to Scotland the same that the sap is to the tree, which, being taken awaie, the tree must needs die and wither.

"To be briefe, the duke of Excester used such earnest and pithie persuasions to induce the king and the whole assemblie of the parlement to credit his words, that immediatelie after he had made an end, all the companie beganne to crie, *Warre, warre; France, France.* Hereby the bill for dissolving of religious houses was clearlie set aside, and nothing thought on but onelie the recovering of France, according as the archbishop had mooved. . . .

"Immediatelie after, the king sent over into France his uncle the duke of Excester, the lord Greie admerall of England, the archbishop of Dubline, and the bishop of Norwich, ambassadors unto the French king, with five hundred horsse, which were lodged in the temple house in Paris, keeping such triumphant cheere in their lodging, and such a solemne estate in their riding through the citie, that the Parisiens and all the Frenchmen had no small mervell at their honorable port. The French king received them verie honorablie and banketted them right sumptuouslie, shewing to them justs and martiall pastimes, by the space of three days togither, in the which justs the king himselfe, to shew his courage and activitie to the Englishmen, manfullie brake speares and lustilie tournied. When the triumph was ended, the English ambassadors, having a time appointed them to declare their message, admitted to the French kings presence, required of him to deliver unto the king of England the realme and crowne of France, with the entier duchies of Aquiteine, Normandie, and Anjou, with the countries of Poictiou and Maine. Manie other requests they made: and this offered withall, that if the French king would, without warre and effusion of Christian bloud, render to the king their maister his verie right and lawfull inheritance, that he would be content to take in mariage the ladie Katharine, daughter to the French king, and to indow her with all the duchies and countries before rehearsed; and if he would not so doo, then the king of England did expresse and signifie to him, that with the aid of God, and helpe of his people, he would recover his inheritance, wrongfullie withholden from him, with mortall warre, and dint of sword. . . .

" The Frenchmen being not a little abashed at these demands, thought not to make anie absolute answer in so weightie a cause, till they had further breathed; and therefore praied the English ambassadors to saie to the king their maister, that they now having no opportunitie to conclude in so high a matter, would shortlie send ambassadors into England, which should certifie and declare to the king their whole mind, purpose, and intent. The English ambassadors returned with this answer, making relation of everie thing that was said or doone. King Henrie, after the returne of his ambassadors, determined fullie to make warre in France, conceiving a good and perfect hope to have fortunate successe, sith victorie for the most part followeth where right leadeth, being advanced forward by justice, and set foorth by equitie." . . .

A.D. 1415.—" When king Henrie had fullie furnished his navie with men, munition, and other provisions, perceiving that his capteines misliked nothing so much as delaie, determined his souldiors to go a shipboord and awaie. But see the hap, the night before the daie appointed for their departure, he was crediblie informed, that Richard earle of Cambridge, brother to Edward duke of York, and Henrie lord Scroope of Masham, lord treasuror, with Thomas Graie, a knight of Northumberland, being confederat togither, had conspired his death; wherefore he caused them to be apprehended. The said lord Scroope was in such favour with the king, that he admitted him sometime to be his bed-fellow, in whose fidelitie the king reposed such trust, that when anie privat or publike councell was in hand, this lord had much in the determination of it. For he represented so great gravitie in his countenance, such modestie in behaviour, and so vertuous zeale to all godlinesse in his talke, that whatsoever he said was thought for the most part necessarie to be doone and followed. Also the said sir Thomas Greie (as some write) was of the kings privie councell.

" These prisoners upon their examination, confessed, that for a great summe of monie which they had received of the French king, they intended verelie either to have delivered the king alive into the hands of his enimies, or else to have murthered him before he should have arrived in the duchie of Normandie. When king Henrie had heard all things opened, which he desired to know, he caused all his nobilitie to come before his presence, before whome he caused to be brought the offendors also, and to them said. Having thus conspired the death and destruction of me, which am the head of the realme and governour of the people, it maie be (no doubt) but that you likewise have sworne the confusion of all that are here with me, and also the desolation of your owne countrie. To what horror (O Lord) for any true English hart to consider, that such an execrable iniquitie should ever so bewrap you, as for pleasing of a forren enimie to imbrue your hands in your bloud, and to ruine your owne native soile. Revenge herein touching my person, though I seeke not; yet for the safegard of you, my deere freends, and for due preservation of all sorts, I am by office to cause example to be shewed. Get ye hence, therefore, ye poore miserable wretches, to the receiving of your just reward, wherein Gods majestie give you grace of his mercie and repentance of your heinous offenses. And so immediatelie they were had to execution. . . . Diverse write that Richard earle of Cambridge did not conspire with the lord Scroope and Thomas Graie for the murthering of king Henrie to please the French king withall, but onelie to the intent to exalt to the crowne his brother in law Edmund earle of March as heire to Lionell duke of Clarence: after the death of which earle of March, . . . the earle of Cambridge was sure that the crowne should come to him by his wife, and to his children, of hir begotten. And therefore (as was thought) he rather confessed himselfe for need of monie to be corrupted by the French king, than he would

declare his inward mind, and open his verie intent and secret purpose. . . .

"But now to proceed with king Henries dooings. After this, when the
wind came about prosperous to his purpose, he caused the mariners to
weie up anchors, and hoise up sailes, and to set forward with a thousand
ships, on the vigil of our ladie daie the Assumption, and tooke land at
Caur, commonlie called Kideaux, where the river Saine runneth into the
sea, without resistance. . . . The French king being advertised that king
Henrie was arrived on that coast, sent in all haste the lord de la Breth
constable of France, the seneshall of France, the lord Bouciqualt marshall of France, the seneshall of Henault, the lord Lignie, with other,
which fortified townes with men, victuals, and artillerie, on all those
frontiers towards the sea. And hearing that Harflue was besieged, they
came to the castell of Caudebecke, being not farre from Harflue, to the
intent they might succour their freends which were besieged, by some
policie or meanes; but the Englishmen, notwithstanding all the damage
that the Frenchmen could worke against them, foraied the countrie,
spoiled the villages, bringing manie a rich preie to the campe before
Harflue. And dailie was the towne assaulted; for the duke of Glocester, to whome the order of the siege was committed, made three mines
under the ground, and approching to the wals with his engins and or-
dinance, would not suffer them within to take anie rest. For although
they with their countermining somewhat disappointed the Englishmen,
and came to fight with them hand to hand within the mines, so that they
went no further forward with that worke; yet they were so inclosed on
ech side, as well by water as land, that succour they saw could none
come to them. . . .

"The capteins within the towne, perceiving that they were not able
long to resist the continuall assaults of the Englishmen, knowing that
their wals were undermined, and like to be overthrowne (as one of their
bulwarks was alredie, where the earles of Huntington and Kent had set
up their banners) sent an officer at armes foorth about midnight after the
feast daie of saint Lambert, which fell that yeare upon the tuesdaie, to
beseech the king of England to appoint some certeine persons as commissioners from him, with whome they within might treat about some
agreement. The duke of Clarence, to whome this messenger first declared his errand, advertised the king of their request, who granting
thereto, appointed the duke of Excester with the lord Fitz Hugh, and
sir Thomas Erpingham, to understand their minds, who at the first re-
quested a truce untill sundaie next following the feast of saint Michaell,
in which meane time, if no succour came to remoove the siege, they
would undertake to deliver the towne into the kings hands, their lives
and goods saved. The king advertised hereof, sent them word, that except they would surrender the towne to him the morow next insuing,
without anie condition, they should spend no more in talke about the
matter. . . .

"The king, neverthelesse was after content to grant a respit upon certeine conditions, that the capteins within might have time to send to the
French king for succour (as before ye have heard) lest he intending

greater exploits, might lose time in such small matters. When this com-
position was agreed upon, the lord Bacquevill was sent unto the French
king, to declare in what point the towne stood. To whome the Dolphin
answered, that the kings power was not yet assembled in such number
as was convenient to raise so great a siege. This answer being brought
unto the capteins within the towne, they rendered it up to the king of
England, after that the third daie was expired. . . . All this done, the
king ordeined capteine to the towne his uncle the Duke of Excester, who
established his lieutenant there, one sir John Fastolfe, with fifteene hundred men, or (as some have) two thousand and thirtie six knights, whereof the baron of Carew, and sir Hugh Lutterell, were two councellors. . . .

"King Henree, after the winning of Harflue, determined to have pro-
ceeded further in the winning of other townes and fortresses ; but because the dead time of the winter approched, it was determined by advise
of his councell, that he should in all convenient speed set forward, and
march through the countrie towards Calis by land, least his returne as
then homewards should of slanderous toongs be named a running awaie ;
and yet that journie was adjudged perillous, by reason that the number
of his people was much minished by the flix and other fevers, which sore
vexed and brought to death above fifteene hundred persons of the armie ;
and this was the cause that his returne was the sooner appointed and
concluded. . . .

"At length the king approched the river of Some, and finding all the
bridges broken, he came to the passage of Blanchetake, where his great
grandfather king Edward the third a little before had stricken the battell
of Cressie ; but the passage was now so impeached with stakes in the
botome of the foord, that he could not passe, his enimies besides there
awaie so swarming on all sides. He therefore marched forwards to
Arames, marching with his armie, and passing with his carriage in so
martial a maner, that he appeared so terrible to his enimies, as they
durst not offer him battell. And yet the lord Dalbreth constable of
France, the marshall Boncequault, the earl of Vendosme great master of
France, the duke of Alanson, and the earle of Richmont, with all the
puissance of the Dolphin laie at Abuile, but ever kept the passages, and
coasted aloofe, like a hauke though eager yet not hardie on her preie.
The king of England kept on his journie till he came to the bridge of
saint Maxence, where he found above thirtie thousand Frenchmen, and
there pitched his field, looking suerlie to be fought withall. . . .

"The king the same daie found a shallow, between Corbie and Peron,
which never was espied before, at which he with his army and carriages
the night insuing, passed the water of Some without let or danger, and
therewith determined to make haste towards Calis, and not to seeke for
battell, except he were thereto constreined, because that his armie by
sicknesse was sore diminished, in so much that he had but onelie two
thousand horssemen, and thirteen thousande archers, bilmen, and of all
sorts of other footmen.

"The Englishmen were brought into some distresse in this jornie, by
reason of their vittels in maner spent, and no hope to get more ; for the
enimies had destroied all the corne before they came. Rest could they

none take, for their enimies with alarmes did ever so infest them ; dailie it rained, and nightlie it freesed ; of fuell there was great scarsitie, of fluxes plentie ; monie inough, but wares for their releefe to bestow it on, had they none. Yet in this great necessitie, the poor people of the countrie were not spoiled, nor anie thing taken of them without paiment, nor anie outrage or offense done by the Englishmen, except one, which was, that a souldiour tooke a pix out of a church, for which he was apprehended, and the king not once remooved till the box was restored, and the offendoor strangled. The people of the countries thereabout, hearing of such zeale in him to the maintenance of justice, ministred to his armie victuals, and other necessaries, although by open proclamation so to doo they were prohibited.

"The French king being at Rone, and hearing that king Henrie was passed the river of Some, was much displeased therewith, and assembling his councell, to the number of five and thirtie, asked their advise what was to be done. There was amongst these five and thirtie, his sonne the Dolphin, calling himselfe king of Sicill ; the dukes of Berrie and Britaine, the earl of Pontieu the kings yoongest sonne, and other high estates. At length thirtie of them agreed that the Englishmen should not depart unfought withall, and five were of a contrarie opinion, but the greater number ruled the matter ; and so Montjoy king at armes was sent to the king of England to defie him as the enimie of France, and to tell him that he should shortlie have battell. King Henrie advisedlie answered : Mine intent is to doo as it pleaseth God, I will not seeke your maister at this time ; but if he or his seeke me, I will meet with them God willing. If anie of your nation attempt once to stop me in my journie now towards Calis, at their jeopardie be it ; and yet will not anie of you so unadvised, as to be the occasion that I die your tawnie ground with your red bloud. When he had thus answered the herald, he gave him a princelie reward, and licence to depart. Upon whose returne, with this answer, it was incontinentlie on the French side proclaimed, that all men of warre should resort to the constable to fight with the king of England. Whereupon, all men apt for armor and desirous of honour, drew them toward the field. The Dolphin sore desired to have beene at the battell, but he was prohibited by his father ; likewise Philip earle of Charolois would gladlie have beene there, if his father the duke of Burgognie would have suffered him : manie of his men stale awaie, and went to the Frenchmen. The king of England hearing that the Frenchmen approched, and that there was an other river for him to passe with his armie by a bridge, and doubting least if the same bridge should be broken, it would be greatlie to his hinderance, appointed certeine capteins with their bands, to go thither with all speed before him, and to take possession thereof, and so to keepe it, till his comming thither. . . .

"The cheefe leaders of the French host were these : the constable of France, the marshall, the admerall, the lord Rambures maister of the crosbowes, and other of the French nobilitie, which came and pitched downe their standards and banners in the countie of saint Paule, within the territorie of Agincourt, having in their armie (as some write) to the number of threescore thousand horssemen, besides footmen, wagoners and other. They were lodged even in the waie by the which the Englishmen must needs passe towards Calis, and all that night after their comming thither made great cheare and were verie merie, pleasant, and full of game. The Englishmen also for their parts were of good comfort, and nothing abashed of the matter, and yet they were both hungrie, wearie, sore travelled, and vexed with manie cold diseases. Howbeit, reconciling themselves with God by hoosell and shrift, requiring assistance at his hands that is the onelie giver of victorie, they determined rather to die, than to yeeld, or flee. The daie following was the five and twentieth of October in the year 1415, being then fridaie, and the feast of Crispine and Crispinian, a day faire and fortunate to the English, but most sorrowfull and unluckie to the French. . . .

" When he had thus ordered his battels, he left a small companie to keepe his campe and cariage, which remained still in the village, and then calling his capteins and soldiers about him, he made to them a right grave oration, mooving them to plaie the men, whereby to obteine a glorious victorie, as there was hope certeine they should, the rather if they would but remember the just cause for which they fought, and whome they should incounter, such faint-harted people as their ancestors had so often overcome. To conclude, manie words of courage he uttered, to stirre them to doo manfullie, assuring them that England should never be charged with his ransome, nor anie Frenchman triumph over him as a captive: for either by famous death or glorious victorie would he (by Gods grace) win honour and fame.

" It is said that as he heard one of the host utter his wish to another thus : I would to God there were with us now so manie good soldiers as are at this houre within England ! the king answered : I would not wish a man more here than I have ; we are indeed in comparison to the enimies but a few, but if God of his clemencie doo favour us, and our just cause (as I trust he will) we shall speed well inough. But let no man ascribe victorie to our owne strength and might, but onelie to Gods assistance, to whome I have no doubt we shall worthilie have cause to give thanks therefore. And if so be that for our offenses sakes we shall be delivered into the hands of our enimies, the lesse number we be, the lesse damage shall the realme of England susteine ; but if we should fight in trust of multitude of men, and so get the victorie (our minds being prone to pride), we should thereupon peradventure ascribe the victorie not so much to the gift of God, as to our owne puissance, and thereby provoke his high indignation and displeasure against us ; and if the enimie get the upper hand, then should our realme and countrie suffer more damage and stand in further danger. But be you of comfort, and show your selves valiant, God and our just quarrell shall defend us, and deliver these our proud adversaries with all the multitude of them which you see, (or at least the most of them), into our hands. . . . The Frenchmen in the meane while, as though they had beene sure of victorie, made great triumph, for the capteins had determined before how to divide the spoile, and the soldiers the night before had plaid the Englishmen at dice. The noble men had devised a chariot, wherein they might trium-

phantlie conveie the king captive to the citie of Paris, crieng to their
soldiers ; Haste you to the spoile, glorie, and honor ; little weening
(God wot) how soone their brags should be blowne awaie.

"Here we maie not forget how the French thus in their jolitie, sent a
herald to king Henrie, to inquire what ransome he would offer. Where-
unto he answered, that within two or three houres he hoped it would so
happen, that the Frenchmen should be glad to common rather with the
Englishmen for their ransoms, than the English to take thought for their
deliverance, promising for his owne part, that his dead carcasse should
rather be a prize to the Frenchmen, than his living bodie should paie
anie ransome. When the messenger was come backe to the French
host, the men of warre put on their helmets, and caused their trumpets
to blow to the battell. They thought themselves so sure of victorie, that
diverse of the noble men made such hast towards the battell, that they
left manie of their servants and men of warre behind them, and some
of them would not once staie for their standards ; as amongst other the
duke of Brabant, when his standard was not come, caused a baner to
be taken from a trumpet and fastened to a speare, the which he commanded to be borne before him insteed of his standard. . . .

"And so about foure of the clocke in the after noone, the king, when
he saw no appearance of enimies, caused the retreit to be blowen ; and
gathering his armie togither, gave thanks to almightie God for so happie
a victorie, causing his prelats and chapleins to sing this psalm, *In exitu
Israel da Aegypto*, and commanded everie man to kneele downe on the
grounde at this verse : *non nobis Domine, non nobis, sed nomini tuo da
gloriam*. Which doone, he caused *Te Deum*, with certeine anthems to
be soong, giving laud and praise to God, without boasting of his owne
force or anie humane power. That night he and his people tooke rest,
and refreshed themselves with such victuals as they found in the French
campe, but lodged in the same village where he laie the night before.

"In the morning Montjoie king at armes and foure other French heralds came to the K. to know the number of prisoners, and to desire
buriall for the dead. Before he made them answer (to understand wha
they would saie) he demanded of them whie they made to him that request, considering that he knew not whether the victorie was his or theirs.
When Montjoie by true and just confession had cleered that doubt to the
high praise of the king, he desired of Montjoie to understand the name of
the castell neere adjoining : when they had told him it was called Agincourt, he said, Then shall this conflict be called the battell of Agincourt.* . . .

"It was no marvell though this battell was lamentable to the French
nation, for in it were taken and slaine the flower of all the nobilitie of

---

* Agincourt, or Azincour, is about twenty miles south of Saint-Omer, a station on the
railway from Calais to Paris. Of the "castell neere adjoining" only the foundations
now remain. The hottest of the fight raged between Azincour and the neighbouring
commune of Trammecour, where a wood still exists corresponding to that in which
Henry is said to have posted his archers, who contributed so much to the victory.

The battle-field of Crécy (see ii. 4. 54) is only about twenty miles from that of Agincourt, being some twelve miles from Abbeville, on the route from Boulogne to Paris.
The windmill from which Edward III. watched the battle is still standing.

France. There were taken prisoners, Charles duke of Orleance, nephue to the French king, John duke of Burbon, the lord Bouciqualt one of the marshals of France (he after died in England) with a number of other lords, knights, and esquiers, at the least fifteene hundred, besides the common people. There were slaine in all of the French part to the number of ten thousand men, whereof were princes and noble men bearing baners one hundred twentie and six; to these, of knights, esquiers, and gentlemen, so manie as made up the number of eight thousand and foure hundred (of the which five hundred were dubbed knights the night before the battell) so as of the meaner sort, not past sixteene hundred. Amongst those of the nobilitie that were slaine, these were the cheefest, Charles lord de la Breth high constable of France, Jaques of Chatilon lord of Dampier admerall of France, the Lord Rambures master of the crossebowes, sir Guischard Dolphin great master of France, John duke of Alanson, Anthonie duke of Brabant brother to the duke of Burgognie, Edward duke of Bar, the earle of Nevers an other brother to the duke of Burgognie, with the erles of Marle, Vaudemont, Grandpree, Roussie, Fauconberge, Fois and Lestrake, beside a great number of lords and barons of name. Of Englishmen, there died at this battell, Edward duke of Yorke, the earle of Suffolke, sir Richard Kikelie, and Davie Gamme esquier, and of all other not above five and twentie persons, as some doo report. . . .

"The king, like a grave and sober personage, and as one remembering from whom all victories are sent, seemed little to regard such vaine pompe and shewes as were in triumphant sort devised for his welcomming home from so prosperous a journie, in so much that he would not suffer his helmet to be caried with him, whereby might have appeared to the people the blowes and dints that were to be seene in the same; neither would he suffer anie ditties to be made and soong by minstrels of his glorious victorie; for that he would wholie have the praise and thanks altogither given to God." . . .

A.D. 1420.— "Whilest these victorious exploits were thus happilie atchived by the Englishmen, and that the king laie still at Rone, in giving thanks to almightie God for the same, there came to him eftsoones ambassadours from the French king and the duke of Burgognie to moove him to peace. The king minding not to be reputed for a destroier of the countrie, which he coveted to preserve, or for a causer of Christian bloud still to be spilt in his quarrell, began so to incline and give ear unto their sute and humble request, that at length (after often sending to and fro) and that the bishop of Arras and other men of honor had beene with him, and likewise the earle of Warwike, and the bishop of Rochester had beene with the duke of Burgognie, they both finallie agreed upon certeine articles, so that the French king and his commons would thereto assent. Now was the French king and the queene with their daughter Katharine at Trois in Champaigne governed and ordered by them, which so much favoured the duke of Burgognie, that they would not, for anie earthlie good, once hinder or pull backe one jot of such articles as the same duke should seeke to preferre. And therefore what needeth manie words, a truce tripartite was accorded betweene the two kings and the duke, and their countries, and order taken that the king of England should send in the companie of the duke of Burgognie his ambassadours into Trois in Champaigne, sufficientlie authorized to treat and conclude of so great a matter. The king of England, being in good hope that all his affaires should take good successe as he could wish or desire, sent to the duke of Burgognie his uncle, the duke of Excester, the earle of Salisburie, the bishop of Elie, the Lord Fanhope, the lord Fitz Hugh, sir John Robsert, and sir Philip Hall, with diverse doctors, to the number of five hundred horsse, which in the companie of the duke of Burgognie came to the citie of Trois the eleventh of March. The king, the queene, and the ladie Katharine them received, and hartilie welcomed, shewing great signes and tokens of love and amitie. After a few daies they fell to councell, in which at length it was concluded that king Henrie of England should come to Trois, and marie the ladie Katharine ; and the king hir father after his death should make him heire of his realme, crown and dignitie. . . .

"King Henrie being informed by them of that which they had doone, was well content with the agreement, and with all diligence prepared to go unto Trois. . . . The duke of Burgognie accompanied with many noble men, received him two leagues without the towne, and conveied him to his lodging. All his armie was lodged in small villages thereabout. And after that he had reposed himselfe a little, he went to visit the French king, the queene, and the ladie Katharine, whome he found in saint Peters church, where was a verie joious meeting betwixt them (and this was on the twentith daie of Maie) and there the king of England, and the ladie Katharine were affianced."*

---

* Saint Peter's Church, or the Cathedral of Troyes, was begun in the early part of the 13th century, the choir being completed about A.D. 1250. The nave was added in the beginning of the 14th century; and the west front, which was never completed, was begun in 1506. The interior has been admirably restored in our day, under the direction of M. Viollet-le-Duc. The windows retain much of their original glass, which is remarkable for its beauty and brilliancy.

The marriage of Henry and Katherine took place on the 2d of June, 1420, not in the cathedral where they had been affianced, but in the Church of Saint John, which was built in the 14th century. It is still standing, though in a comparatively ruinous condition. Within the church is a well which furnishes water to the people of that quarter of the city.

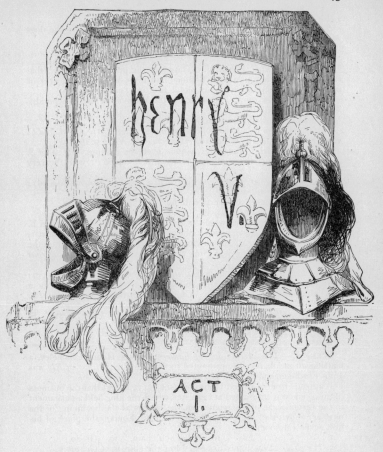

PROLOGUE.—The folio has "Enter Prologue;" but see line 32 : "Admit me *Chorus*," etc.

1, 2. Warb. sees here an allusion to the Peripatetic system with its several heavens, "the highest of which was one of fire ;" but, as Douce remarks, the poet "simply wishes for poetic fire and a due proportion of inventive genius."

Invention is metrically a quadrisyllable.   Gr. 479.

7. *Leash'd in like hounds*, etc.   Cf. *J. C.* iii. 1. 273 : " let slip the dogs of war ;" and 1 *Hen. VI.* iv. 2. 10 :

> "You tempt the fury ot my three attendants,
> Lean famine, quartering steel, and climbing fire."

Holinshed says that Henry V. declared to the people of Rouen " that the goddesse of battell, called Bellona, had three handmaidens, ever of necessitie attending upon her, as blood, fire, and famine."

9. *Flat, unraised spirit*.   " Opposed to the Muse of fire, etc." (Schmidt) The folio has " spirits."

12. *Vasty*.   For similar adjectives, see Gr. 450.

13. *This wooden O*.   The Globe theatre (see cut, p. 131).   Cf. *A. and C.* v. 2. 81 : " The little O, the earth."   See also *M. N. D.* p. 165.

The very casques.   The mere casques, even the casques.   Cf. *T. of S.* iv. 3. 32 : " the very name of meat :" *Rich. III.* i. 4. 60 : " with the very noise," etc.

14. *Affright the air*.   Steevens quotes Prudentius, *Psychomachia*, 297 : " clypeo dum territat auras."

16. *Attest*.   " Serve as a certificate for " (Schmidt) ;   stand for.

18. *Imaginary*.   Imaginative.   Gr. 3.

22. *Perilous*.   Steevens would make this an adverb (=very), as in B. and F., *Humorous Lieutenant:* "She is perilous crafty," etc. ; but it is clearly an adjective.   M. Mason cites *M. of V.* iii. 1. 4 : " wracked on the *narrow seas*—the Goodwins, I think they call the place—a very *dangerous* flat," etc.

25. *Puissance*.   Army ; as in ii. 2. 190 below.   Cf. *K. John*, iii. 1. 339 : " draw our puissance together."   S. makes the word a dissyllable or a trisyllable, as suits the measure.   Cf. iii. prol. 21 below, and 2 *Hen. IV.* ii. 3. 52.

30. *Accomplishment*.   Work, performance ; as in *R. of L.* 716.   S. uses the word only twice.

31. *The which*.   See Gr. 270.

SCENE I.—The *Archbishop of Canterbury* was Henry Chicheley, a Carthusian monk, recently promoted to that see ; the *Bishop of Ely* was John Fordham, consecrated in 1388.

It appears from Hall and Holinshed (see p. 132 above) that the business of this scene was transacted at Leicester, where the king held a parliament in the second year of his reign ; but the chorus at the beginning of the next act shows that the poet intended to make London the place of his first scene (Malone).

1. *Self*.   Cf. *C. of E.* v. 1. 10 : " that self chain," etc.   Gr. 20.

3. *Was like*.   Was likely to pass.   For the ellipsis, cf. Gr. 397.

4. *Scambling*.   Scrambling.   Cf. v. 2. 196 below.   See also *Much Ado*, v. 1. 94 and *K. John*, iv. 3. 146.   Steevens and Halliwell give many examples of the word from writers of the time.

5. *Question*.   Debate, consideration.   Cf. ii. 4. 17 below.

15. *Lazars*.   Diseased beggars, lepers.   Cf. *T. and C.* ii. 3. 36 and v. 1. 72.

16. *Corporal.* Corporeal. See *Macb.* p. 162.

26. *Mortified.* Killed. See *Macb.* p. 247.

28. *Consideration,* etc. "As paradise, when sin and Adam were driven out by the angel, became the habitation of celestial spirits, so the king's heart, since *consideration* has driven out his follies, is now the receptacle of wisdom and of virtue" (Johnson).

33. *In a flood.* Alluding, as Johnson thinks, to the cleansing of the Augean stables by Hercules, who turned a river through them.

34. *Currance.* Current (compare *concurrence, occurrence,* etc.). The later folios substitute "currant" or "current."

35. *Nor never.* For the double negative, see Gr. 406.

36. *All at once.* "And all the rest, and everything else" (Schmidt). Cf. *A. Y. L.* iii. 5. 36 :

> "Who might be your mother,
> That you insult, exult, and all at once,
> Over the wretched?"

St. says it was a trite phrase in the time of S., and quotes F. Sabie, *Fisherman's Tale,* 1594 : "She wept, she cride, she sob'd, and all at once ;" and Middleton, *Changeling,* iv. 3 : "Does love turn fool, run mad, and all at once ?"

43. *List.* For the transitive use, see Gr. 199.

47. *Familiar.* Used adverbially. Gr. 1. For *so* omitted before *that,* see Gr. 283.

48. *The air,* etc. "This line is exquisitely beautiful" (Johnson). Malone quotes *A. Y. L.* ii. 7. 48 :

> "I must have liberty
> Withal, as large a charter as the wind,
> To blow on whom I please."

51. *Practic.* Practical. Used by S. nowhere else. *Theoric* (=theory) occurs in *A. W.* iv. 3. 162 and *Oth.* i. 1. 24. The meaning of the passage, as Johnson remarks, is "that his theory must have been taught by art and practice ; which, says he, is strange, since he could see little of the true art or practice among his loose companions, nor ever retired to digest his practice into theory." On the "redundant object" in 53, see Gr. 414.

55. *Companies.* Companions. The use of the word here favours Theobald's emendation of *M. N. D.* i. 1. 219.

57. *Never noted.* For the ellipsis, see Gr. 403.

59. *Popularity.* "Vulgarity" (Schmidt) ; "plebeian intercourse" (Steevens). So in the only other instance in which S. uses the word, 1 *Hen. IV.* iii. 2. 69 : "Enfeoff'd himself to popularity."

60. *The strawberry grows,* etc. It was a common opinion in the time of S. that plants growing together imbibed each other's qualities. Sweet flowers were planted near fruit-trees with the idea of improving the flavour of the fruit, while ill-smelling plants were carefully cleared away lest the fruit should be tainted by them. But the strawberry was supposed to be an exception to the rule, and not to be corrupted by the "evil communications" of its neighbours. St. Francis de Sales says : "In tilling our garden we cannot but admire the fresh innocence and

purity of the strawberry, because although it creeps along the ground, and is continually crushed by serpents, lizards, and other venomous reptiles, yet it does not imbibe the slightest impression of poison, or the smallest malignant quality—a true sign that it has no affinity with poison;" and again : "In this manner you may remain innocent amidst the hissing of serpents, and, as a little strawberry, you will not suffer contamination from slimy things creeping near you."

63. *Contemplation.* His serious or thoughtful nature.

66. *Crescive in his faculty.* "Increasing in its proper power" (Johnson). S. uses *crescive* nowhere else ; but he has *crescent* in the same sense in *Ham.* i. 3. 11, *A. and C.* ii. 1. 10, and *Cymb.* i. 4. 2. Steevens quotes Drant's *Horace's Art of Poetry*, 1567 : "As lusty youths of crescive age doe flourishe freshe and grow." On *his* = its, see Gr. 228.

73. *Swaying*, etc. Inclining our way.

76. *Upon.* Used temporally, or perhaps = in pursuance of the decrees passed there (Schmidt).

81. *Withal.* See Gr. 196.

86. *Severals* is explained by Abbott (Gr. 433) as "details." It is opposed to "generals" in *T. and C.* i. 3. 180 : "Severals and generals of grace exact." In *W. T.* i. 2. 226 ("some severals Of head-piece extraordinary") it is = individuals. M. Mason would read "several." *Unhidden* = open, clear. "The *passages* of his *titles* are the *lines* of *succession* by which his claims descend" (Johnson). Schmidt explains *unhidden passages* doubtfully as "open, manifest traces (?)."

SCENE II.—2. *Good uncle.* "The person here addressed was Thomas Beaufort, Earl of Dorset, who was half-brother to King Henry IV., being one of the sons of John of Gaunt by Katharine Swynford. He was not made Duke of Exeter until after the battle of Agincourt, Nov. 14, 1416" (Malone).

3. *Shall we*, etc. The quartos begin the play here.

4. *Be resolv'd.* Be satisfied. Cf. *J. C.* iii. 1. 131, iii. 2. 183, iv. 2. 14, etc.

11. *The law Salique.* See extract from Holinshed, p. 132 above.

15. *Or nicely charge*, etc. "Take heed, lest by nice and subtle sophistry you burthen your knowing soul, or *knowingly burthen your soul*, with the guilt of advancing a false title, or of maintaining, by specious fallacies, a claim which, if shown in its native or true colours, would appear to be false" (Johnson). *Miscreate* = illegitimate. For the form, see Gr. 342 ; and for *with*, Gr. 193.

19. *Approbation.* Proving, establishing. Cf. *T. N.* iii. 4. 198 : "more approbation than ever proof itself would have earned him ;" *Cymb.* i. 4. 134 : "on the approbation of what I have spoke," etc.

21. *Impawn.* Pledge, engage. The meaning appears to be, Take care how you commit us to a policy involving such serious consequences.

27. *Wrong gives.* The folio has "wrongs gives," and in the next line "makes." See Gr. 247.

35. *There is no bar*, etc. How closely this speech follows Holinshed will be seen by comparing it with the chronicle, pp. 132, 133 above.

40. *Gloze.* Also spelled *glose*. It means to explain, though generally

with the added idea of sophistry. Cf. *T. and C.* ii. 2. 165 : "Have gloz'd but superficially;" *Rich. II.* ii. 1. 10: "whom youth and ease have taught to gloze," etc.

46. *Charles the great.* That is, Charlemagne. *Charlemain* in 75 is Charles the Bald, who also assumed the title of Magnus, or Great.

57. *Four hundred one and twenty years.* No commentator has called attention to the error in subtracting 426 from 805, which leaves 379, not 421. S. follows Holinshed, who appears to have taken 405 from 826.

65. *Which.* See Gr. 265 ; and for *of* = from, in 67, Gr. 166.

72. *To fine his title.* The reading of the quarto of 1608 ; the folio has "To find his title." Johnson suggested "To line" (that is, to strengthen, as in *Macb.* i. 3. 112), but afterwards preferred "find" = "to determine in favour of." The Coll. MS. has "found," but Coll. retains *fine*, as W. does, though both favour *line*. To *fine*, as Steevens remarks, is "to make showy or specious." Schmidt prefers *find* = "to trace out."

74. *Convey'd himself as heir.* Managed to be considered the heir. *Convey* often means "to do or manage with secrecy" (Schmidt). See *Macb.* p. 239, note on *Convey your pleasures*.

The Lady Lingare. No such person appears in French history. Ritson remarks that "these fictitious persons and pedigrees seem to have been devised by the English heralds, to 'fine a title with some show of truth' which 'in pure truth was corrupt and naught.'"

77. *The tenth.* It should be *the ninth*, as some modern eds. give it ; but S. wrote *the tenth*, copying the error from Holinshed (see p. 133).

79. *Conscience.* Metrically a trisyllable. Gr. 479.

82. *Lineal of.* Directly descended from.

88. *King Lewis his.* See Gr. 217.

93. *Them.* For the reflexive use, see Gr. 223.

94. *Imbare.* The quarto has "imbace ;" the folio, "imbarre." *Imbare* (=lay open, expose to view) was suggested by Warb. and adopted by Theo. ; also by Halliwell, D., W., and others. K. and the Camb. editors prefer "imbar" (=bar in, secure).

98. *In the book of Numbers.* See *Numb.* xxvii. 8. For the form *writ*, see Gr. 343.

99. *When the man dies.* That is, without a son. The reading is that of the folio ; the quarto has "the sonne," which is followed by some modern eds.

103. *Great-grandsire's.* That is, Edward III.

107. *Defeat on.* Cf. *Ham.* ii. 2. 597 :

> "Upon whose property and most dear life
> A damn'd defeat was made."

108. *Whiles.* See Gr. 137. The allusion here is to the battle of Cressy, as described by Holinshed: "The earle of Northampton and others sent to the king, where he stood aloft on a windmill-hill ; the king demanded if his sonne were slaine, hurt, or felled to the earth. No, said the knight that brought the message, but he is sore matched. Well, (said the king,) returne to him and them that sent you, and saie to them, that they send no more to me for any adventure that falleth, so long as my son is alive; for I will that this journeye be his, with the honour thereof. The slaugh-

ter of the French was great and lamentable at the same battle, fought
the 26th August, 1346."

114. *Cold for action.* Malone explains this "cold for *want of* action"
(Gr. 154). Cf. *Macb.* i. 5. 37 : "dead for breath ;" *Cymb.* iii. 6. 17 : "to
sink for food." K. says : "The unemployed forces, seeing the work
done to their hands, stood laughing by and indifferent for action—*un-
moved to action*."

118. *Renowned them.* Made them famous. Cf. *T. N.* iii. 3. 24 : "that
do renown this city."

119. *Runs.* S. often uses the singular inflection with two singular
nouns as subject. Gr. 336.

126. *So hath*, etc. The *hath* is emphatic ; "your highness hath indeed
what they think and know you have" (Malone).

132. For the measure, see Gr. 463.

137. *Lay down our proportions.* Assign the proper number of troops.
Cf. 304 below, also ii. 4. 45.

139. *Advantages.* This may mean "opportunities," as J. H. explains
it (cf. iii. 6. 112), or "conditions favourable to success," as Schmidt gives
it.

140. *Marches.* Borders, border country. Cf. 3 *Hen. VI.* ii. 1. 140 :
"For in the marches here we heard you were."

142. *Inland.* The quarto has "England," which Coll. quotes in proof
that the "copy" for that ed. was obtained by taking notes of the acted
play.

144. *Intendment.* Intention. Cf. *V. and A.* 222, and *A. Y. L.* i. 1. 140.

145. *Still.* Always. Gr. 69. *Giddy*=excitable. Cf. 2 *Hen. IV.* iv.
5. 214 :
> "Be it thy course to busy giddy minds
> With foreign quarrels."

See also *T. A.* iv. 4. 87 and v. 2. 78. The Coll. MS. substitutes "greedy."

150. *Brim fulness.* Virtually one word (as Schmidt gives it), though
the preceding words compel us to print it as two.

151. *Gleaned.* Exhausted, laid bare (Schmidt), or "drained of soldiers" (J. H.). *Assays*=attacks, incursions.

153. *That.* So that. See on i. 1. 47 above.

154. *At the ill neighbourhood.* The folio reading ; the quarto has "at
the bruit thereof." For *shook*, see Gr. 343.

155. *Fear'd.* Frightened. Cf. *M. of V.* ii. 1. 9 :
> "this aspect of mine
> Hath fear'd the valiant ;"

and see note in our ed. p. 137.

162. *Fame.* The Coll. MS. substitutes "train."

163. *Chronicle.* "The similitude between the chronicle and the sea
consists only in this, that they are both full, and filled with something
valuable" (Johnson). The quarto has "your," the folio "their chronicle ;" *her* is Johnson's emendation.

165. *Sumless.* Inestimable. The quarto has "shiplesse treasurie."
See Gr. 446.

166. The folio gives this speech to the Bishop of Ely, but it appears

from Holinshed that it belongs to the Earl of Westmoreland. **As Warb.** remarks, it is absurd to give it to one of the churchmen in confederacy to push on the king to war with France.

167. *France.* Metrically a dissyllable. Gr. 486.

173. *Tear.* The quarto has "spoile," and the folio "tame." The emendation is Rowe's, and is adopted by Coll., Sr., W., the Cambridge editors, Halliwell, and others.

175. *Curst.* The quarto reading; the folio has "crush'd," which Schmidt explains as "forced, strained." *Curst* = "perverse, froward" (Walker), or "sharp, bitter" (W.).

176. *Safeguard.* Also used as a verb in *Rich. II.* i. 2. 35 : "to safeguard thine own life."

177. *Pretty.* Steevens wished to substitute "petty," but *pretty* is used colloquially in a diminutive sense (Schmidt). Cf. *A. and C.* v. 2. 243, etc.

178. *While that.* On *that* as "a conjunctional affix," see Gr. 287.

179. *Advised.* "Heedful, wary" (J. H.). Cf. *M. of V.* i. 1. 142 : "with more advised watch," etc.

181. *Consent.* Some editors here and in 206 read "concent" (=harmony) ; "a needless emendation," as Schmidt calls it.

182. *Congreeing.* Agreeing. The folio reading ; the quarto has "congrueth."

184. *In.* Into. Gr. 159.

185. *Setting endeavour,* etc. "The sense is, that all endeavour is to terminate in obedience, to be subordinate to the public good and general design of government" (Johnson).

189. *The act of order.* Malone explains this as "the *law* or *statute* of order ;" but it probably means orderly action. Pope changed *act* to "art," as does the Coll. MS.

190. *They have a king,* etc. Malone cites a long passage from Lyly's *Euphues and his England,* which S. may have had in mind. K. remarks : "This is probable ; but, nevertheless, the lines before us are a remarkable instance of the power of S. in the improvement of everything he borrowed. It is not only in the poetic elevation of the description that the improvement consists, but in the rejection of whatever is false or redundant." *Sorts* = different kinds, or degrees.

191. *Correct.* Set things right. Not elsewhere used absolutely by S.

192. *Venture trade.* Johnson compares the phrase "hazard battle."

194. *Make boot upon.* Seek booty in, plunder. Cf. 2 *Hen. VI.* iv. 1. 13 : "make boot of this." In *A. and C.* iv. 1. 9, "make boot of" = take advantage of.

199. *Civil.* "Well-governed, peaceful" (Schmidt).

202. *Sad-eyed.* Sober-looking. For *sad* = grave, serious, see *M. N. D.* p 175.

203. *Executors.* Executioners. For the accent, see Gr. 490. Elsewhere it has the modern accent ; as in *Rich. II.* iii. 2. 148, etc.

210. *In.* Into. See on 184 above.

212. *End.* Here the quarto enables us to correct the misprint "And" of the folio.

220. *Hardiness.* Bravery ; as in *Cymb.* iii. 6. 22 :

> "Plenty and peace breeds cowards; hardness even
> Of hardiness is mother."

S. uses the word only twice.

Policy = "the art of managing public affairs" (Schmidt); as in i. 1. 45 and ii. prol. 14, etc.

221. *Dauphin.* The folio has here, as elsewhere, "Dolphin," which W. retains.

226. *Empery.* Empire, dominion; as in *T. A.* i. 1. 19, 22, 201. It is used in the concrete sense (=country under a prince) in *Rich. III.* iii. 7. 136 and *Cymb.* i. 6. 120.

233. *Waxen.* The folio reading; the quarto has "paper." Either = "easily effaced" (Schmidt). As Hunter remarks, *worshipp'd* is used in the sense of *honoured*, and the passage means "a grave without any inscription, not even one of the meanest and most fugitive."

239. *Or shall we*, etc. That is, shall we spare your feelings and state our message indirectly? Cf. *Rich. III.* iii. 5. 93 :

> "But touch this sparingly, as 't were far off;
> Because you know, my lord, my mother lives."

245. *In few.* In few words, in brief. Cf. *Temp.* i. 2. 144 ; *M. for M.* iii. 1. 237 ; *Ham.* i. 3. 126, etc.

248. For the measure, see Gr. 469.

252. *Galliard.* A lively French dance. Cf. *T. N.* i. 3. 127 : "What is thy excellence in a galliard, knight?" Sir John Davies, in his *Orchestra*, describes the dance thus :

> "But, for more divers and more pleasing show,
>   A swift and wandring daunce she did invent,
> With passages uncertaine, to and fro,
>   Yet with a certaine answere and consent
>   To the quicke musicke of the instrument.
> Five was the number of the musicks feet,
> Which still the daunce did with five paces meet.
> A gallant daunce, that lively doth bewray
>   A spirit, and a vertue masculine,
> Impatient that her house on earth should stay,
>   Since she herselfe is fiery and divine :
>   Oft doth she make her body upward fline ;
> With lofty turnes and capriols in the ayre,
> Which with the lusty tunes accordeth faire."

Halliwell quotes *Lanquettes Chronicle :* "About this time [1541] a new trade of daunsyng galiardes upon five paces, and vaunting of horses, was brought into the realme by Italians, which shortly was exercised commonly of all yonge men, and the old facion lefte."

256. *Desires you let*, etc. For the construction, see Gr. 349, 369.

258. *Tennis-balls.* In the old play of *The Famous Victories of Henry the Fifth* (see p. 10) this present consists of a gilded tun of tennis-balls and a carpet. The answer of King Henry there is as follows :

> "My lord, prince Dolphin is very pleasant with me.
> But tell him, that instead of balls of leather,
> We will toss him balls of brass and of iron :
> Yea, such balls as never were toss'd in France.
> The proudest tennis-court in France shall rue it."

Cf. Drayton's *Battle of Agincourt:*

> "I 'll send him balls and rackets if I live;
> That they such racket shall in Paris see,
> When over line with bandies I shall drive;
> As that, before the set be fully done,
> France may perhaps into the hazard run."

261. *Rackets.* The bat used for striking the ball at tennis. Cf. *2 Hen. IV.* ii. 2. 23.

263. *Shall strike.* For the omission of the relative, see Gr. 244.

266. *Chases.* According to Douce, "a *chace*, at tennis, is that spot where a ball falls, beyond which the adversary must strike his ball to gain a point or *chace.*" It seems to have been often used in this latter sense of a point gained in the game. Cf. Sidney's *Arcadia*, iii. : "Then Fortune (as if she had made chases enow on the one side of that bloody Tenis-court) went on the other side of the line," etc. Halliwell quotes a dialogue from the *Marow of the French Tongue,* 1625, of which the following is part: "I have thirty, and a chase. . . . And I, I have two chases. —Sir, the last is no chase, but a losse."

267. *Comes o'er us.* "Wakes us to sad remembrance" (Schmidt); or, perhaps, simply=reminds us. Cf. *Oth.* iv. 1. 20 : "O, it comes o'er my memory," etc.

269. *This poor seat of England.* The throne. Cf. i. 1. 88 above : "the crown and seat of France." See also *Rich. II.* ii. 1. 120, iii. 2. 119, iv. 1. 218, etc.

270. *Living hence.* Probably = "withdrawing from the court," as Steevens explains it. Cf. *1 Hen. IV.* iii. 2. 32, where the king says to the prince :

> "Thy place in council thou hast rudely lost,
> Which by thy younger brother is supplied,
> And art almost an alien to the hearts
> Of all the court and princes of my blood."

See also *Rich. II.* v. 3. 1, where Henry IV. asks :

> "Can no one tell of my unthrifty son?
> 'T is full three months since I did see him last."

274. *Sail.* For the metaphor, cf. *Sonn.* 86. 1 : "Was it the proud full sail of his great verse," etc. The Coll. MS. substitutes "soul."

276. *For that,* etc. "To qualify myself for this undertaking, I have descended from my station, and studied the arts of life in a lower character" (Johnson).

282. *Gun-stones.* Cannon-balls were at first made of stone. Steevens quotes Holinshed : "About seaven of the clocke marched forward the light pieces of ordinance, with stone and powder." In the *Brut of England,* it is said that Henry "anone lette make tenes balles for the Dolfin in all the haste that they myght, and they were great gonnestones for the Dolfin to playe with alle. But this game at tenes was too rough for the besieged, when Henry playede at the tenes with his hard gonnestones," etc.

292. *Venge.* Not "'venge," as often printed. See *Rich. II.* p. 158.

300. *Happy.* Favourable, propitious ; as often. Cf. *Much Ado,* **iv. 2.** 285 ; *Rich. II.* i. 3. 276, etc.

304. *Proportions.* See on 137 above.

306. *Reasonable.* The Coll. MS. needlessly substitutes "seasonable." Steevens quotes *T. and C.* ii. 2. 44 :

> "if he do set
> The very wings of reason to his heels."

307. *God before.* "God *going* before" (W.). Abbott (Gr. 203) explains it as a case of the preposition transposed. The expression occurs again iii. 6. 147. Johnson there quotes an old *Dialogue between a Herdsman and a Maiden going on a Pilgrimage to Walsingham,* in which the herdsman takes his leave in these words : "Now, go thy ways, and God before."

309. *Task his thought.* Cf. 6 above : "That task our thoughts," etc.

SOUTHAMPTON.

ACT II.

PROLOGUE.—3. *Thrive.* That is, are doing a good business. The Coll. MS. reads "strive."

6. *The mirror,* etc. Cf. 1 *Hen. VI.* i. 4. 74 : "mirror of all martial men ;" *Hen. VIII.* ii. 1. 53 : "The mirror of all courtesy," etc.

8. *For now sits,* etc. Steevens remarks that the idea is taken from the

ancient trophies, in which swords were often encircled with naval or mural crowns. For the personification, cf. Milton, *P. L.* vi. 306 :

> "while Expectation stood
> In horrour."

Henley says that the image is borrowed from a wood-cut in the 1st ed. of Holinshed.

19. *Kind.* True to their nature or kinship ; "not degenerate and corrupt, but such as a thing or person ought to be" (Schmidt) ; nearly equivalent to *natural.* Cf. *M. for M.* iii. 1. 229 : "in his love toward her ever most kind and natural."

21. *Hollow bosoms.* False hearts. Cf. *Hen. VIII.* iii. 1. 104 : "hollow hearts," etc.

23. *Richard earl of Cambridge.* Richard de Coninsbury, younger son of Edmund of Langley, Duke of York. He was father of Richard Duke of York, who was father of Edward IV.

24. *Henry lord Scroop.* Third husband of Joan Duchess of York, mother-in-law of Richard Earl of Cambridge.

26. *The gilt of France.* The gold of France ; the only instance of this sense in S. Steevens quotes *An Alarum for London,* 1602 :

> "To spend the victuals of our citizens,
> Which we can scarcely compass now for gilt."

For the play on *gilt* and *guilt,* cf. 2 *Hen. IV.* iv. 5. 129, and see *Macb.* p. 192.

28. *This grace of kings.* Used in a complimentary sense, like "mirror of all Christian kings" in 6 above. Steevens quotes Chapman's *Homer :*

> "with her the grace of kings,
> Wise Ithacus, ascended ;'"

and again :

> "Idæus, guider of the mules, discern'd this grace of men."

31, 32. The folio reads :

> "Linger your patience on, and wee 'l digest
> Th' abuse of distance ; force a play :" etc.

The passage is "evidently corrupt" (Schmidt), and perhaps hopelessly so. *Well,* suggested by Pope, is generally adopted ; and many editors accept his reading of the next line, "The abuse of distance, *while we* force a play." The Coll. MS. has "*and so* force a play." K. believes that the lines were meant to be erased. Steevens explains *force a play* as "to produce a play by compelling many circumstances into a narrow compass." *Force* is used by S. in the sense of *farce* (=stuff, as in "force-meat" still) in *T. and C.* ii. 3. 232 and v. 1. 64.

35. *Gentles.* Gentlefolk. Compare *L. L. L.* iv. 2. 172 : "the gentles are at their game." It is usually a vocative, as here. Cf. *L. L. L.* ii. 1. 225 ; *M. N. D.* v. 1. 128, 436 ; *M. W.* iii. 2. 92, etc.

40. *We 'll not offend,* etc. "That is, you shall pass the sea without the qualms of sea-sickness" (Johnson).

41. *Till the king come,* etc. The meaning evidently is that the scene is not to be changed to Southampton until the king makes his appear-

ance; but there seems to be a "confusion of construction." Cf. Gr. 409–416. Of the emendations suggested, Hanmer's "But *when* the king *comes* forth" is the only one worth mentioning.

SCENE I.—2. *Lieutenant Bardolph.* Some commentators would make Bardolph a "corporal," and not a "lieutenant;" but, as K. remarks, they overlook the tone of authority which he uses both to Pistol and Nym. It appears from an old MS. in the British Museum, that Wm. Pistail and R. Bardolf were among the cannoniers serving in Normandy in 1435.

3. *Ancient.* Corrupted from *ensign.* In 1 *Hen. IV.* iv. 2. 34 it meant the standard.

5. *Smiles.* Farmer suggested "smites" (also in the Coll. MS.), which W. adopts. Malone says: "Perhaps Nym means only to say, I care not whether we are friends at present; however, when time shall serve, we shall be in good humour with each other: but be it as it may."

18. *Troth-plight.* Betrothed. It is also an adjective in *W. T.* v. 3. 151: "Is troth-plight to your daughter." In *W. T.* i. 2. 278 it is a noun.

22. *A tired mare.* Steevens quotes Pierce's *Supererogation:* "Silence is a slave in a chain, and patience the common pack-horse of the world."

26. *Tike.* Cur. Cf. *Lear,* iii. 6. 73 : "Or bobtail tike."

33. *Drawn.* The folio has "hewn." Theo. suggested *drawn,* which is adopted by the Camb. editors, D., W., and others. Halliwell retains *hewn,* which some explain as = drunk. *Lady* refers to the Virgin Mary.

39. *Iceland.* The folio has "Island," the quarto "Iseland." Steevens quotes *Ram-Alley,* 1611 : "A baboon, a parrot, and an Izeland dog;" and *Two Wise Men,* etc., 1619 : "these Iceland dogs." Halliwell says that Fleming in his *English Dogges,* 1576, mentions "Iseland dogges, curled and rough all over."

42. *Shog.* "Nym's word for *jog*" (Schmidt). Halliwell quotes examples of it from B. and F., and other writers of the time. *Solus* is of course the Latin for alone.

44. *Mervailous.* The folio reading, probably = "marvellous," which many eds. substitute for it. Schmidt calls it "an unintelligible word."

46. *Perdy.* A corruption of *par Dieu.* Cf. *C. of E.* iv. 4. 74 ; *Ham.* iii. 2. 305, etc.

49. *I can take.* The quarto has "talk," which Malone prefers. As K. suggests, *I can take* may mean, as in modern slang, "I understand you; I know what you are about."

51. *Barbason.* A demon; also mentioned in *M. W.* ii. 2. 311. "The unmeaning tumour of Pistol's speech very naturally reminds Nym of the sounding nonsense uttered by conjurers" (Steevens).

59. *Exhale.* The commentators are in doubt whether this means "draw your sword" or "die." Either makes sense—if it be necessary to make Pistol speak sense.

68. *Couple a gorge!* The folio reading, which some editors think it necessary to change to good French, "Coupe la gorge;" though, as we see in iv. 4, Pistol has but a poor smattering of that language.

70. *Hound of Crete.* Malone thinks that here is an insinuation that

Nym "thirsted for blood," as the Cretan hounds "appear to have been bloodhounds;" but as Steevens sagely remarks, "Pistol on the present, as on many other occasions, makes use of words to which he had no determinate meaning."

71. *Spital*. Hospital; as in the London *Spitalfields*. It occurs again in v. 1. 73. *Powdering tub* refers to the treatment of certain diseases by sweating in a heated tub.

73. *The lazar kite*, etc. Steevens quotes Gascoigne, *Dan Bartholomew of Bathe*, 1587 : "Nor seldom seene in kites of Cressid's kind;" and Greene, *Card of Fancy*, 1601 : "What courtesy is to be found in such kites of Cressid's kind?" In *The Forrest of Fancy*, 1579, we find "any catte of Cressid's kind."

95. *Compound*. Agree, come to terms. Cf. iv. 3. 80 and iv. 6. 33 below.

116. *Quotidian tertian*. The dame jumbles together the *quotidian* fever, the paroxysms of which recurred daily, and the *tertian*, in which the period was three days.

121. *Fracted*. Broken. Cf. *T. of A*. ii. 1. 22 : "his fracted dates." Strange to say, no critic has attempted to make sense of *corroborate*.

124. *Lambkins*. Cf. 2 *Hen. IV*. v. 3. 121 : "thy tender lambkin now is king." The folio has "for (Lambekins) we will liue ;" and some modern eds. give "for, lambkins, we," etc. *Condole* is used by S. only here and in Bottom's blundering talk in *M. N. D*. i. 2. 29, 43.

SCENE II.—1. *Fore*. Usually printed "'fore" in the modern eds. We follow the early eds. and Schmidt in giving it *fore*. It occurs often in S.

2. *By and by*. Presently, soon ; as often in S. Cf. *V. and A*. 347 :

> "But now her cheek was pale, and by and by
> It flash'd forth fire, as lightning from the sky;"

T. G. of V. i. 3. 85 :

> "The uncertain glory of an April day,
> Which now shows all the beauty of the sun,
> And by and by a cloud takes all away."

Ham. iii. 2. 391 :

> "*Polonius*. My lord, the queen would speak with you, and presently.
>
> . . . .
>
> *Hamlet*. Then I will come to my mother by and by," etc.

See also *Matt*. xiii. 21 and *Luke*, xxi. 9.

8. *His bedfellow*. S. here follows Holinshed (see p. 135 above). Steevens quotes *A Knack to Know a Knave*, 1594 : "Yet, for thou wast once bedfellow to a king," etc. *Bedfellow* was common as a familiar appellation among the nobility in olden time.

15. *Powers*. Forces. S. uses both the singular and the plural in this sense. See *J. C*. p. 168, note on *Are levying powers*.

23. *Nor leave not*. See Gr. 406.

31. *Create*. For the form, see Gr. 342. Cf. *miscreate*, i. 2. 16.

33. *Shall forget*, etc. Perhaps S. had in mind *Psalms*, cxxxvii. 5 (Steevens).

36. *Steeled sinews*. Cf. iv. 1. 274 : "steel my soldiers' hearts."

43. *His more advice.* "His return to more coolness of mind" (Johnson). The Coll. MS. has "our" for *his*, but no change is called for. Cf. *M. of V.* iv. 2. 6 : "upon more advice" (that is, upon reflection) ; *M. for M.* v. 1. 469 : "after more advice," etc. Gr. 17.

44. *Security.* Carelessness, confidence. Cf. *J. C.* ii. 3. 8 : "security gives way to conspiracy ;" *Macb.* iii. 5. 32 : "security Is mortals' chiefest enemy," etc.

46. *By his sufferance.* By tolerating him. Cf. *Cor.* iii. 1. 24 : "Against all noble sufferance," etc.

53. *Heavy orisons.* Weighty petitions. Cf. *Cymb.* i. 3. 32 : "to encounter me with orisons," etc.

54. *Proceeding on distemper.* "Committed in the state of drunkenness" (Schmidt). Cf. Gr. 180. *Distemper* often means mental derangement or excitement—in this case, due to intoxication. Cf. *Oth.* i. 1. 99 : "Full of supper and distempering draughts." Steevens quotes Holinshed : "gave him wine and strong drink in such excessive sort, that he was therewith distempered and reeled as he went."

55. *How shall we,* etc. "If we may not *wink* at small faults, *how wide must we open our eyes* at great ?" (Johnson).

61. *Late.* Lately appointed ; as in ii. 4. 31 below it means lately sent. The Coll. MS. substitutes "state."

74. *Paper.* That is, white as paper. Cf. *Macb.* v. 3. 16 : "those linen cheeks of thine."

75. *Cowarded.* Not elsewhere used by S. as a verb. Gr. 290.

79. *Quick.* Living. Cf. *Ham.* v. 1. 137 : "'t is for the dead, not for the quick," etc. See also *Acts,* x. 42 ; *2 Tim.* iv. 1 ; *Heb.* iv. 12, etc.

87. *Appertinents.* Used by S. as a noun only here. We have the adjective in *L. L. L.* i. 2. 17 and *2 Hen. IV.* i. 2. 194.

95. *Ingrateful.* Used by S. oftener than *ungrateful.* **Gr. 442.**

98. *Coin'd me into gold.* Cf. *J. C.* iv. 3. 72 :

> "By heaven, I had rather coin my heart,
> And drop my blood for drachmas," etc.

102. *Annoy.* Harm. Cf. *J. C.* i. 3. 22 : "without annoying me," etc.

103. *Stands off,* etc. Stands out as distinctly, etc.

106. *Either's.* Each other's. Cf. *Temp.* i. 2. 450 : "They are both in either's powers," etc.

107. *Grossly.* "Palpably ; with a plain and visible connection of cause and effect" (Johnson). For *cause* the Coll. MS. has "course."

108. *That admiration,* etc. That they excited no exclamation of surprise. Boswell quotes *A. Y. L.* iii. 2. 203 : "wonderful, and after that, out of all whooping !"

113. *Voice.* Verdict, judgment. Cf. *M. of V.* iv. 1. 356 : "'gainst all other voice," etc.

117. *Glistering.* S. does not use *glisten.* See *Mer.* p. 145.

118. *Temper'd.* Fashioned, moulded. Cf. *T. G. of V.* iii. 2. 64, etc.

122. *Lion gait.* Cf. *1 Pet.* v. 8.

123. *Vasty Tartar.* On *vasty,* cf. i. prol. 12 and ii. 4. 105 ; and on *Tartar* = Tartarus, *T. N.* ii. 5. 225 and *C. of E.* iv. 2. 32.

127. *Affiance.* Confidence. Cf. *Cymb.* i. 6. 163. "One of the worst

consequences of breach of trust is the diminution of that confidence which makes the happiness of life, and the dissemination of suspicion, which is the poison of society" (Johnson).

Show. Appear. Cf. *V. and A.* 366 ; *R. of L.* 252, 395 ; *M. of V.* ii. 2. 193, iv. 1. 196, etc.

134. *In modest complement.* "That is, in a corresponding outward appearance" (Schmidt). St. makes *complement* = "accomplishments, perfection, completeness ; applied sometimes to mental, sometimes to physical attainments, and occasionally, as here, merely to the taste and elegance displayed in dress." He quotes a note of Drayton's upon the *Epistle from Geraldine to Lord Surrey:* "but Apparell and the outward Appearance intituled *Complement.*" The modern distinction of *complement* and *compliment* is not found in the early eds. of S., the former being the only orthography.

135. *Not working,* etc. Not trusting the air or look of any man till he had tried him by enquiry and conversation (Johnson).

136. *And but in purged judgment,* etc. And trusting neither eye nor ear except after careful scrutiny of the reasons for doing so.

137. *Bolted.* Sifted, refined. Cf. *Cor.* iii. 1. 322 : "bolted language."

139. *To mark,* etc. The folio has "To make." The emendation is due to Theo.

Full-fraught and best indued=most gifted and most richly endowed. Gr. 398. For the thought, cf. *Cymb.* iii. 4. 63 :

> "so thou, Posthumus,
> Wilt lay the leaven on all proper men ;
> Goodly and gallant shall be false and perjur'd
> From thy great fall."

147. *Henry.* The quarto reading ; the folio has "Thomas," which is wrong.

151. *Discover'd.* Uncovered, disclosed. Gr. 439.

159. *Which.* As to which. Gr. 272. *Sufferance*=suffering ; or "death by execution" (Schmidt).

165. *My fault,* etc. Reed quotes the words of Parry, a conspirator against Queen Elizabeth : "Discharge me *a culpa,* but not *a pœna,* good ladie."

169. *Earnest.* Earnest money ; "a part paid beforehand as a pledge" (Schmidt). Cf. *W. T.* iv. 4. 659 : "Indeed, I have had earnest ; but I cannot with conscience take it," etc.

175. *Tender.* Cherish, take care of. Cf. *Rich. II.* i. 1. 32 : "Tendering the precious safety of my prince," etc.

176. *You have sought.* The quarto reading ; the 1st folio omits *have,* and the later folios have "you three sought."

181. *Dear.* Grievous. See *Rich. II.* p. 164, or *Temp.* p. 124.

188. *Rub.* Obstacle, impediment. Cf. *Rich. II.* iii. 4. 4 : "the world is full of rubs ;" and see note in our ed. p. 197.

190. *Puissance.* See on i. prol. 25.

191. *Expedition.* March. Cf *J. C.* iv. 3. 170 : "Bending their expedition toward Philippi," etc.

192. *Cheerly*. Cheerfully, gladly. Cf. *Temp.* i. 1. 6 : "Cheerly, cheerly, my hearts !" *Rich. II.* i. 3. 66 : "cheerly drawing breath," etc.

The signs of war = banners. On *advance*, cf. *L. L. L.* iv. 3. 367 : "Advance your standards ;" *K. John*, ii. 1. 207 : "These flags of France, that are advanced here," etc.

SCENE III.—1. *Honey-sweet*. Cf. *T. and C.* iii. 1. 71 : "honey-sweet lord ;" *Id.* iii. 1. 154 : "honey-sweet queen."

Bring thee = accompany thee. Cf. *W. T.* iv. 3. 122 : "Shall I bring thee on the way ?" See also *Gen.* xviii. 16 ; *Acts*, xxi. 5 ; 2 *Cor.* i. 16, etc.

3. *Yearn*. Grieve, mourn. The word is "erne" in the 1st and 2d folios, "yern" in the 3d and 4th. See *J. C.* p. 153, note on *The heart of Brutus yearns to think upon*.

8. *Arthur's bosom*. Mrs. Quickly is not strong on Scripture.

9. *Finer*. Johnson thought this a blunder for *final*, but it is more likely = *fine*, as Malone and Schmidt make it.

10. *Christom*. A blunder for *chrisom*. The chrisom was the white vesture put upon the child after baptism, and worn until the mother came to be churched. Blount, in his *Glossography*, 1678, says that *chrisoms* in the bills of mortality are such children as die within the month of birth, because during that time they were to wear the *chrisom cloth*.

12. *The turning o' the tide*. Alluding to the old notion that nobody dies except at the ebb of the tide.

15. *A' babbled of green fields*. The folio has "a Table of greene fields." The emendation is Theobald's, and is generally adopted. W. calls it "the most felicitous conjectural emendation ever made of Shakespeare's text." It is sustained by the preceding "play with flowers." Various other corrections have been suggested, but they are hardly worth mentioning.

19. *A' should not think of God*. Malone suggests that S. may have been indebted to the following story in *Wits, Fits, and Fancies*, 1595 : "A gentlewoman fearing to be drowned, said, now Jesu receive our soules ! Soft, mistress, answered the waterman ; I trow, we are not come to that passe yet."

23. *Upward and upward*. W. prints "up'ard, and up'ard," and says, "Thus the original, very characteristically." But the folio has "vppeer'd, and vpward ;" and the quarto, "vpward, and vpward."

25. *Of sack*. For *of* = about, concerning, see Gr. 174.

30. *Carnation*. Mrs. Quickly confounds *incarnate* and *carnation ;* but the former was sometimes used for the latter. Henderson quotes *Questions of Love*, 1566 : "Yelowe, pale, redde, blue, whyte, graye, and incarnate ;" and Reed adds from the *Inventory of the Furniture to be provided for the Reception of the Royal Family, at the Restoration*, 1660 : "the rich incarnate velvet bed ;" and again : "his majesty's incarnate velvet bed."

41. *Pitch and pay*. A proverbial expression of the time. Steevens quotes several examples of it ; as from *Blurt Master Constable*, 1602 : "will you pitch and pay, or will your worship run ?" Farmer adds from Florio : "Pitch and paie, and go your waie."

44. *Hold-fast*, etc. Alluding to the old proverb, " Brag is a good dog, but hold-fast is a better " (Douce).

45. *Caveto.* Take care, be cautious. The quarto has "cophetua."

46. *Clear thy crystals.* Dry thine eyes; though Johnson thought it might better mean "wash thy glasses."

SCENE IV.—1. *Comes.* For the singular form, see Gr. 335.

2. *More than carefully.* " With more than common care " (Johnson).

5. *Make forth.* Go forth. Cf. *J. C.* v. 1. 25 : "Make forth ; the generals would have some words," etc.

7. *Line.* Strengthen, fortify. Cf. *Macb.* i. 3. 112 : "did line the rebel ;" and see note in our ed. p. 164. See also on i. 2. 72 above.

9. *England.* The King of England. Cf. *K. John*, iii. 4. 8 : "And bloody England into England gone," etc. See *Macb.* p. 239.

11. *Fits.* Befits, becomes. Cf. *T. G. of V.* i. 1. 81 : "A silly answer and fitting well a sheep," etc.

13. *Fatal and neglected.* " Fatally neglected, neglected to our destruction " (Schmidt).

16. *Dull.* Make inert and careless. Cf. *Oth.* ii. 3. 394 : "Dull not device by coldness and delay."

18. *Musters.* Levies of troops. For the arrangement, cf. *M. N. D.* iii. 1. 113, 114 ; *Ham.* iii. 1. 151 ; *Macb.* i. 3. 60, etc.

20. *As were.* See Gr. 107.

25. *A Whitsun morris-dance.* An ancient dance in which the performers were dressed in grotesque costume, with bells, etc. For a full description of it, see Douce's *Illustrations of Shakespeare.*

26. *King'd.* Furnished with a king. In *Rich. II.* v. 5. 36 it is=made a king. Steevens quotes Warner's *Albion's England*, viii. 42 : " and king'd his sister's son."

28. *Humorous.* Capricious. In *K. John*, iii. 1. 119 Fortune is called " her humorous ladyship."

31. *Question your grace.* For the "optative subjunctive," see Gr. 364.

34. *In exception.* In taking exception, making objections. Cf. 1 *Hen. IV.* i. 3. 78 ; *Ham.* v. 2. 242, etc.

35. *Constant.* Firm, unshaken ; as in ii. 2. 133 above. Cf. *J. C.* iii. 1. 22 : "Cassius, be constant ;" *Id.* iii. 1. 60 : "constant as the northern star," etc.

36. *Forespent.* Past. In *Cymb.* ii. 3. 64, it is=previously bestowed ; and in 2 *Hen. IV.* i. 1. 37, exhausted.

37, 38. Malone compares *R. of L.* 1807 :

> " Brutus, who pluck'd the knife from Lucrece' side,
> Seeing such emulation in their woe,
> Began to *clothe his wit* in state and pride,
> Burying in Lucrece' wound his *folly's show.*
> He with the Romans was esteemed so
>   As silly-jeering idiots are with kings,
>   For sportive words and uttering foolish things.

> " But now he throws that *shallow habit* by,
> Wherein deep policy did him disguise,
> And arm'd his long-hid wits advisedly.
> To check the tears in Collatinus' eyes."

Boswell remarks that the best commentary on the passage will be found in Prince Henry's soliloquy in 1 *Hen. IV.* i. 2. 219–241.

46. *Projection.* Projecting, plan, calculation. Cf. Gr. 451. The construction is somewhat confused, but the meaning, as Malone suggests, evidently is, "which proportions of defence, when weakly and niggardly projected, resemble a miser who spoils his coat," etc.

50. *Hath been flesh'd.* Hath preyed. Cf. 2 *Hen. IV.* iv. 5. 133:

> "the wild dog
> Shall flesh his tooth on every innocent."

For *of him*=his, see Gr. 225. Cf. 64 below.

51. *Strain.* Lineage, race. Cf. *J. C.* v. 1. 39: "the noblest of thy strain;" *T. of A.* i. 1. 259:

> "The strain of man's bred out
> Into baboon and monkey."

53. For *much,* see Gr. 51.

54. *Was struck.* Schmidt compares *Cymb.* v. 5. 468: "the stroke of this battle." Steevens quotes the title of one of Sir David Lyndsay's poems: "How king Ninus began the first warres and strake the first battell."

55. *Captiv'd.* S. does not use the verb elsewhere. Gr. 290.

57. *His mountain sire.* Theo. would read "mounting"=high-minded, aspiring. The Coll. MS. has "mighty." Steevens quotes Spenser, *F. Q.* i. 11. 4:

> "Where stretcht he lay upon the sunny side
> Of a great hill, himselfe like a great hill."

As Malone remarks, the repetition of *mountain* is much in the poet's manner. See *Macb.* p. 250, note on *Stuff'd bosom of that perilous stuff.*

64. *Fate.* "Great good fortune ordained by destiny" (Schmidt). Cf. *A. and C.* iii. 13. 169: "I will oppose his fate."

70. *Most spend their mouths.* "That is, *bark;* the sportsman's term" (Johnson). Cf. *V. and A.* 695: "Then do they spend their mouths." See also *M. N. D.* iv. 1. 128 and 1 *Hen. VI.* ii. 4. 12.

72. *Good my sovereign.* See Gr. 13.

80. *Longs.* Not "'longs," as often printed. See *Hen. VIII.* p. 162, note on *Longing.* For the singular form, see Gr. 247.

85. *Sinister.* For the accent, see Gr. 490. *Awkward* = "perverse, unbecoming" (Schmidt).

88. *Line.* Pedigree; as it is called two lines below.

90. *Overlook.* Look over, read. Cf. *Ham.* iv. 6. 13: "when thou shalt have overlooked this," etc.

91. *Evenly.* "In a straight line, directly" (Schmidt). Cf. 1 *Hen. IV.* iii. 1. 103: "In a new channel, fair and evenly."

99. *Fiery.* The folio has "fierce," an easy misprint for "fierie." Walker made the correction, which is adopted by D., W., and others.

101. *Will compel.* See Gr. 311 and 348.

103. For "*to* omitted and inserted," see Gr. 350.

105. *Vasty.* See on ii. 2. 123; and for the use of *and,* Gr. 95.

113. *For us.* As for us. Gr. 149.

124. *Womby.* See Gr. 450.

125. *Chide your trespass.* That is, sound it abroad, proclaim it aloud.

Cf. *Temp*. iii. 3. 99 : "it did bass my trespass." For *chiding*=resounding, cf. *Hen. VIII*. iii. 2. 197 : "the chiding flood." See also 1 *Hen. IV*. iii. 1. 45 : "the sea That chides the banks of England," etc.

126. *Ordinance*. Ordnance. Cf. *K. John*, ii. 1. 218, and see extract from Holinshed, p. 136 above. In iii. prol. 26, where the word is a dissyllable, the folio has "Ordenance ;" so "Ordinance" in *Ham*. v. 2. 281. But we find "Ordnance" in *T. of S*. i. 2. 204 and 1 *Hen. VI*. i. 4. 15.

132. *Louvre*. According to some writers the ancient palace of the Louvre was built in the 7th century. What is now called the "Old Louvre" was begun in 1528 under Francis I., and completed by Henry II. in 1548.

137. *Masters*. Possesses. Cf. *Sonn*. 106. 8 : "Even such a beauty as you master now ;" *M. of V*. v. 1. 174 : "the wealth That the world masters," etc.

143. *Footed*. Landed. Cf. *Lear*, iii. 3. 14 and iii. 7. 45.

HEIGHTS BETWEEN HAVRE AND HARFLEUR.

ACT III.

PROLOGUE.—*With imagin'd wing*. With the speed of imagination. Cf. *M. of V*. iii. 4. 52 : "with imagin'd speed."

L

4. *Well appointed.* Well furnished, well equipped. Cf. 1 *Hen. IV.*
i. 1. 190, iv. 1. 25, etc.

Hampton pier. The folio has "Douer peer," which is an obvious error.
See ii. prol. 30, 34, 42.

5. *His royalty.* His majesty. Cf. *L. L. L.* v. 2. 670 ; *W. T.* i. 2. 15 ;
K. John, v. 2. 129, etc.

6. *Fanning.* The folio has "fayning ;" corrected by Rowe. Cf. *Macb.*
i. 2. 49 :

> "Where the Norweyan banners flout the sky
> And fan our people cold."

10. *Threaden.* Cf. *L. C.* 33 : "her threaden fillet."

11. *With.* By. See Gr. 193. The Coll. MS. has "Blown" for *Borne*.

14. *Rivage.* Bank, shore (Fr. *rivage*). Cf. Spenser, *F. Q.* iv. 6. 20 :

> "The which Pactolus with his waters shere
> Throwes forth upon the rivage round about him nere."

17. *Harfleur.* The folio has here, as elsewhere, "Harflew."

18. *Sternage.* "Stern, steerage" (Schmidt). Holinshed has the verb
stern=steer ; and Chapman the noun=rudder. See Wb.

21. *Puissance.* For the pronunciation, see on i. prol. 25. On *pith*=
strength, cf. *Oth.* i. 3. 83 and *Ham.* iii. 1. 86.

30. *To dowry.* On *to*=for, see Gr. 189.

32. *Likes not.* Pleases not. Cf. iv. 3. 77 : "Which likes me better,"
etc. Gr. 297.

33. *Linstock.* "The staff to which the match is fixed when the ordnance is fired" (Johnson). In the stage-direction that follows, *chambers*=small cannon. Cf. 2 *Hen. IV.* ii. 4. 57 : "the charged chambers."
See *Hen. VIII.* p. 9. On *devilish cannon*, cf. Spenser, *F. Q.* i. 7. 13 :
"that divelish yron Engin."

35. *Eke.* In the folio "eech." In *M. of V.* iii. 2. 23, we have "ich."
In *Per.* iii. prol. 13, it rhymes with *speech*. W. believes, however, that in
this case *speech* was pronounced like *speak*, and not *eke* like *each*.

SCENE I.—7. *Summon.* Rowe's correction of the "commune" of the
early eds.

8. *Hard-favour'd.* Hard-featured, ill-looking. Cf. *V. and A.* 133 :
"Were I hard-favour'd, foul, or wrinkled-old," etc.

9. *Aspect.* For the accent, see Gr. 490.

10. *Portage.* Port-hole.

11. *O'erwhelm.* Lower above. Cf. *V. and A.* 183 : "His louring
brows o'erwhelming his fair sight," etc.

13. *Jutty.* Project beyond. Used by S. as a verb nowhere else.
Confounded = wasted, wave-worn. Cf. *Temp.* ii. 1. 120 : "wave-worn
basis." On *confound*=destroy, see *Macb.* p. 189.

14. *Swill'd with.* Swallowed by. S. uses *swill* only here and in *Rich.
III.* v. 2. 9 :

> "The wretched, bloody, and usurping boar,
>   That spoil'd your summer fields and fruitful vines,
>   Swills your warm blood," etc.

On *ocean*, see Gr. 479.

15. *Now set the teeth.* Cf. *Cor.* i. 3. 70 and *A. and C.* iii. 13. 181.

16. *Bend up*, etc. "A metaphor from the bow" (Johnson). Cf. *Macb.* i. 7. 79.

17. *Noble.* The 1st folio has "noblish;" the later folios "noblest," which some modern eds. adopt. K. has "nobless."

18. *Fet.* Fetched. Cf. Spenser, *F. Q.* v. 3. 11 : "soone the prisoner fet." The 1st folio has "fet" in *Rich. III.* ii. 2. 121. "Deep-fet" occurs in 2 *Hen. VI.* ii. 4. 33, and "far-fet" in *Id.* iii. 1. 293.

21. *Argument.* Matter, business in hand (Schmidt). Cf. *T. and C.* i. 1. 95 : "I cannot fight upon this argument," etc.

31. *Slips.* Nooses in which the dogs were held until started for the game. Cf. Gascoigne, *Absent Lady's Complaint* :

"The greyhound is aggreev'd, although he see his game,
If still in slippe he must be stayde, when he would chase the same."

To *let slip* was to loose the hound from the slip. Cf. 1 *Hen. IV.* i. 3. 278 : "Before the game's afoot thou still let'st slip." See also *Cor.* i. 6. 39 and *J. C.* iii. 1. 273.

SCENE II.—3. *A case of lives.* A pair of lives ; as a *case* of pistols.

4. *Plain-song.* In music "the simple melody, without any variations." Cf. *M. N. D.* iii. 1. 134 and *Hen. VIII.* i. 3. 45.

18. *Preach.* The folio has "breach" here, and elsewhere it is not uniform in marking the peculiarities of Fluellen's pronunciation. None of the modern editors have made this perfectly consistent throughout, and we have not attempted to do it. Capell remarks : "The poet thought it sufficient to mark his [Fluellen's] diction a little, and in some places only ; and the man of taste will be of the same opinion."

19. *Duke.* Perhaps = commander (Latin *dux*), as Malone explains it. See *M. N. D.* p. 125. More likely it is a bit of Pistol's peculiar English.

Men of mould. "Men of *earth*, poor mortal men," as Johnson and Schmidt explain it. W. understands it to mean men "of large frame, and so of strength, of prowess."

22. *Bawcock.* "A term of endearment, synonymous to *chuck*, but always masculine" (Schmidt). Cf. iv. 1. 44 below ; also *T. N.* iii. 4. 125 and *W. T.* i. 2. 121.

25. *Swashers.* Braggarts, bullies. Used by S. nowhere else ; but we have *swashing* = swaggering, in *A. Y. L.* i. 3. 122 and *R. and J.* i. 1. 70.

28. *Antics.* Buffoons, fools. See *Rich. II.* iii. 2. 162 ; *T. and C.* v. 3. 86, etc.

29. *White-liver'd.* Cowardly. Cf. *M. of V.* iii. 2. 86 : "livers white as milk." See *Macb.* p. 249, note on *lily-liver'd.*

38. *Call it purchase.* "This was the cant term for money gained by cheating, as we learn from Greene's *Art of Coneycatching*" (Boswell).

42. To *carry coals* meant "to endure affronts" (Johnson). Cf. *R. and J.* i. 1. 1 : "we'll not carry coals." Nares says that the phrase arose from the fact that the carriers of wood and coals were esteemed the very lowest of menials, the *servi servorum.*

43. *Handkerchers.* The folio has "Hand-kerchers" here, as in sundry other places ; but "Handkerchiefe" in *Oth.* iv. 1. 10, 18, 22, etc.

49. *Fluellen.* An approximation to the Welsh pronunciation of *Llewellyn.*

56. *Plow up.* That is, blow up.

76. *God-den.* Good evening; as in *K. John,* i. 1. 185 ; *Cor.* ii. 1. 103, etc. Cf. *Macb.* p. 175, note on *God 'ield. Pioners* in 78 = pioneers.

93. *Quit you.* Requite you, answer you ; or, perhaps, " tell you also interesting things " (Schmidt). Cf. *Rich. II.* v. 1. 43 :

> " to quit their grief,
> Tell thou the lamentable tale of me," etc.

103. *By the mess.* That is, by the mass.

110. *Of my nation,* etc. The folio gives the passage thus : " Of my Nation ? What ish my Nation ? Ish a Villaine, and a Basterd, and a Knaue, and a Rascall. What ish my Nation ? Who talkes of my Nation ?" K. suggested that there had been an accidental transposition of the type here, and corrected it as in the text. The change, as W. remarks, is supported by the fact that while the other clauses are marked as interrogations, the transposed clause has a period after it. St. thinks, however, that " the incoherence of the original was designed to mark the impetuosity of the speaker."

SCENE III.—2. *Parle.* Parley. Cf. *Rich. II.* i. 1. 192 ; *K. John,* ii. 1. 205, etc.

5. On the measure, see Gr. 503.

10. *The gates of mercy.* Cf. *3 Hen. VI.* i. 4. 177 : " Open thy gate of mercy, gracious Lord !" As Steevens notes, Gray has borrowed the expression in his *Elegy,* 68 : " And shut the gates of mercy on mankind."

11. *Flesh'd.* " Fierce, hardened " (Schmidt). Cf. *Rich. III.* iv. 3. 6 : " flesh'd villains, bloody dogs."

14. *Fresh-fair.* On " compound adjectives," see Gr. 2. In this case the hyphen is not in the folio, and might perhaps as well be omitted.

17, 18. *All fell feats,* etc. " All the savage practices naturally concomitant to the sack of cities " (Johnson).

24. *Bootless.* Used adverbially ; as in *M. N. D.* ii. 1. 37, *J. C.* iii. 1. 75, etc.

26. *Precepts.* For the accent, see Gr. 490. According to Schmidt, the accent is on the first syllable when the word means " instruction, lesson ;" on the second when it means " mandate, summons." This is the only case in which the latter sense occurs in verse. We have it in prose in *2 Hen. IV.* v. 1. 14.

28. *Take pity of.* For the preposition, see Gr. 174 ; and cf. 45 below.

29. *Whiles.* See Gr. 137.

31. *O'erblows.* Blows over, or away. Cf. *Rich. II.* iii. 2. 190 : " This ague-fit of fear is overblown ;" *T. of S.* v. 2. 3 : " scapes and perils overblown," etc.

32. *Heady.* " Impetuous, precipitate " (Schmidt). Cf. i. 1. 34 above ; also *1 Hen. IV.* ii. 3. 58 and *Lear,* ii. 4. 111. The 1st folio has " headly " here ; the later folios, " headdy " or " heady." Malone suggested " deadly," which W. adopts.

35. *Defile.* Rowe's emendation for the "Desire" of the folio. It is also found in the Coll. MS.

Jewry. Judea. Cf. *Rich. II.* ii. 1. 55, etc. See also *John*, vii. 1.

43. *In defence.* That is, in keeping up your resistance.

46. *Returns us.* Sends us back word. Cf. *Rich. II.* iii. 3. 121 : " say thus the king returns," etc. For *powers*=forces, cf. ii. 2. 15 above.

54. *For.* See Gr. 149.

58. *Address.* Prepared, ready. Cf. *J. C.* iii. 1. 29 : " He is address'd," and see note in our ed. p. 156. Steevens quotes Heywood, *Brazen Age*, 1613 : " these champions are addrest for war."

SCENE IV.—Warb. considered this scene "ridiculous," and Hanmer rejected it. Johnson says : " The scene is indeed mean enough when it is read ; but the grimaces of two French women, and the odd accent with which they uttered the English, made it divert on the stage. It may be observed that there is in it not only the French language, but the French spirit. Alice compliments the princess upon her knowledge of four words, and tells her that she pronounces like the English themselves. The princess suspects no deficiency in her instructress, nor the instructress in herself. Throughout the whole scene there may be found French servility and French vanity." W. remarks : " Shakespeare sought to enliven his History by humour ; and his intention here was to excite mirth by the exhibition of a Frenchwoman in the ridiculous emergency of sudden preparation for amorous conquest of an Englishman. This could best be done by making her attempt to learn his language, in doing which she must of course speak French ; and Shakespeare here, as in the subsequent scene between Pistol and the French soldier, instinctively preserved dramatic propriety at the expense of the mere verbal consistency of his work. That the scene is Shakespeare's the promise in the epilogue to 2 *Hen. IV.*, that in the continuation of the story the audience shall be made 'merry with fair Katherine of France,' is sufficient evidence, as Tyrwhitt remarked. Shakespeare's design was known to the writer of that epilogue."

The French is very blunderingly printed in the quarto, but is quite correct in the folio.

SCENE V.—1. The folio has here the stage-direction, " *Enter the King of France, the Dolphin, the Constable of France, and others.*" To the speeches beginning with lines 10 and 30 it prefixes " *Brit.*" But the Duke of " Britaine" does not appear elsewhere in the play, and the editors generally follow Theo. in substituting Bourbon. The stage-direction in the quarto is "*Enter King of* France *Lord Constable, the Dolphin, and* Burbon" (given incorrectly in the notes of the Camb. ed.) ; and " *Bur.*" is prefixed to the first of these speeches, the second being omitted in the quarto. The Camb. ed. remarks : " In Holinshed (p. 1077, ed. 1577), the Dukes of Berry and Britaine are mentioned as belonging to the French king's council, and not the Duke of Bourbon. Shakespeare probably first intended to introduce the Duke of Britaine, and then changed his mind, but forgot to substitute *Bour.* for *Brit.* before the two speeches."

2. *Withal.* "The emphatic form of *with.*" See **Gr. 196.**

6. *Luxury.* Lust; the only meaning of the word in S. Cf. *M. W.* v. 5. 98; *Ham.* i. 5. 83, etc.

7. *Savage.* Uncultivated (Johnson).

9. *Overlook.* Look down on, tower above. For a different sense, see ii. 4. 90 above.

12. *But.* See Gr. 126.

13. *Slobbery.* "Wet and foul" (Schmidt). S. uses the word only here; but we find the verb *slubber* in *Oth.* i. 3. 227 and *M. of V.* ii. 8. 39, and *beslubber* in 1 *Hen. IV.* ii. 4. 341.

14. *Nook-shotten.* Warb. and Schmidt make this = shooting out into capes and necks of land; K. and W. think it more probably means "thrust into a corner apart from the rest of the world"—the "*penitus toto divisos orbe Britannos*" of Virgil. Halliwell compares "cup-shotten" = full of cups, intoxicated.

19. *Sur-rein'd.* Over-ridden. S. uses the word only here. Steevens quotes *Jack Drum's Entertainment*, 1601 : "A sur-rein'd jaded wit, but he rubs on." There is an allusion to the custom of giving horses over-ridden or feverish a *mash ;* that is, a mixture of ground malt and hot water.

Barley broth. A contemptuous term for beer.

31. *Lavoltas.* A kind of dance, in which there was much lofty caper-ing. Cf. *T. and C.* iv. 4. 88 : "Nor heel the high lavolt." It is thus described by Sir John Davies in his *Orchestra :*

> "Yet is there one the most delightful kind,
>   A lofty jumping, or a leaping round,
>   Where arm in arm, two dancers are entwin'd,
>   And whirl themselves in strict embracements bound,
>   And still their feet an anapest do sound:
>   An anapest is all their musick's song,
>   Whose first two feet is short, and third is long.

> "As the victorious twins of Leda and Jove,
>   That taught the Spartans dancing on the sands
>   Of swift Eurotas, dance in heaven above,
>   Knit and united with eternal hands,
>   Among the stars their double image stands,
>   Where both are carried with an equal pace,
>   Together jumping in their turning race."

The *coranto,* or *corranto* (from the Italian *correre,* Latin *currere,* to run), was also a lively dance. Davies says of it :

> "What shall I name those *current* traverses,
>   That on a triple dactyl foot do run,
>   Close by the ground, with sliding passages,
>   Wherein that dancer greatest praise hath won
>   Which with best order can all order shun :
>   For every where he wantonly must range,
>   And turn and wind with unexpected change."

Cf. *A. W.* ii. 3. 49 : "he's able to lead her a coranto ;" *T. N.* i. 3. 137 : "go to church in a galliard, and come home in a coranto."

33. *And that.* On *that,* see Gr. 285.

37. *More sharper.* See Gr. 11.

38. *Delabreth.* S. follows **Holinshed**'s spelling of the name, the modern *D'Albret.*

43. *Foix.* Capell's emendation for the "Loys" of the folio. The latter was not the name of any French family of distinction at that time.

44. *Knights.* The folio has "kings;" corrected by Theo. Cf. iv. 8. 85 below: "princes, barons, lords, knights, squires."

45. *Quit you.* Free or clear yourselves. Cf. ii. 2. 166 above; also *2 Hen. VI.* iii. 2. 218, etc.

47. *Pennons.* Schmidt thinks that the meanings of wing and flag are here combined.

50. *Void his rheum.* Cf. *M. of V.* i. 3. 118: "did void your rheum upon my beard." Steevens quotes *Fur. Bibac. ap. Hor.:* "Juppiter hibernas cana nive conspuit Alpes."

53. *Rouen.* Spelt "Roan" in the early eds., which probably indicates the English pronunciation of the time. Cf. Holinshed's "Rone," p. 138 above.

58. *For achievement.* For the exploit (Schmidt). Malone explains it: "*instead* of achieving a victory over us;" and Abbott refers to Gr. 148.

SCENE VI.—2. *The bridge.* The reference here is to an historical fact. After Henry had passed the Somme, the French attempted to break down the only bridge over the Ternoise, at Blangy, and thus cut off his passage to Calais; but Henry, learning their design, sent forward troops who put the French to flight, and guarded the bridge until the English had crossed.

11. *An aunchient.* See on ii. 1. 3, and cf. 28, 47, and 50 below. The folio reads "an aunchient Lieutenant," the quarto "an Ensigne."

24. *Buxom.* "Lively, fresh, brisk" (Schmidt). S. uses the word only here; unless we are to add *Per.* prol. 23: "buxom, blithe, and full of face." Cf. Milton, *L'All.* 24: "buxom, blithe, and debonair." Spenser uses it in the sense of yielding, obedient; as in *F. Q.* i. 11. 37: "the buxome aire;" *Id.* iii. 2. 23: "Of them that to him buxome are and prone." For the derivation, see Wb.

26. *That goddess blind*, etc. Ritson quotes *The Spanish Tragedy*, 1594:
"Fortune is blind—
Whose foot is standing on a rolling stone."

29. *Muffler.* Apparently here=a bandage over the eyes. In *M. W.* iv. 2. 73, 81, 205, it means "a wrapper worn by women and covering the face" (Schmidt).

37. *A pax.* Altered to "pix" by Theo. Johnson says the two words mean the same, but this is not true. The *pax*, according to Nares, was "a symbol of peace, which, in the ceremony of the mass, was given to be kissed at the time of the offering." In Capt. Stevens's *Spanish Dict.*, we are told that it was the cover of the sacred chalice. The *pix* was the box or shrine in which the consecrated wafers were kept; and the word is still used in the same sense. Cf. Longfellow, *Nuremberg:* "In the church of sainted Lawrence stands a pix of sculpture rare," and see the author's note on the line. Steevens quotes Stowe's *Chronicle:* "palmes, chalices, crosses, vestments, pixes, paxes, and such like." In the pres-

ent passage, S. follows Holinshed, who says (see p. 138 above) that "a souldiour tooke a *pix* out of a church," etc. ; but, as the two words were often confounded, it does not seem worth while to change the folio reading.

54. *Figo.* The Spanish word for *fig;* often used as a term of contempt. For a full discussion of the origin and various meanings thereof, see Douce's *Illustrations of Shakespeare.* In *The fig of Spain* just below, Steevens sees an allusion to the use of poisoned figs, and quotes several passages in support of that explanation ; as from Shirley, *The Brothers*, 1652 : "I must poison him ; one fig sends him to Erebus ;" Ben Jonson, *Every Man in His Humour :* "The lye to a man of my coat is as ominous a fruit as the fico," etc. But the phrase here is probably a mere repetition of the contemptuous *figo.*

61. *See in a summer's day.* Cf. *M. N. D.* i. 2. 75, and see note in our ed. p. 135.

67. *Learn you.* For the expletive use of the pronoun, see Gr. 220.

68. *Sconce.* Bulwark. In *C. of E.* ii. 2. 37, it is applied in jest to a covering for the head (Schmidt).

72. *New-tuned.* The Coll. MS. has "new-coined." W. thinks it should probably be "new-found." Cf. *T. G. of V.* iv. 4. 134 : "new-found oaths."

A beard of the general's cut. Certain professions and classes seem to have been distinguished by the cut of the beard. Thus we read of the *bishop's beard*, the *judge's*, the *soldier's*, the *citizen's*, etc. St. quotes Greene, *Quip for an Upstart Courtier*, 1592 : "he [the barber] descends as low as his beard, and asketh whether he please to be shaven or no ? whether he will have his peak cut short and sharp, amiable, like an inamorato, or broade pendante, like a spade, to be terrible, like a warrior and soldado ?"

75. For *on*=of, see Gr. 182 ; and for *mistook*, just below, Gr. 343.

81. *From the pridge.* That is, about the bridge.

86. *Passages.* Acts, occurrences. Cf. *T. N.* iii. 2. 77 : "such impossible passages of grossness ;" *Cymb.* iii. 4. 94 :

> "It is no act of common passage, but
> A strain of rareness," etc.

96. *Bubukles.* "A corrupt word, formed half of *carbuncle*, half of *bubo*, probably meaning a red pimple" (Schmidt). Steevens quotes Chaucer, *C. T.* 623 :

> "A Sompnour was ther with us in that place,
> That hadde a *fyr-reed* [fire-red] cherubynes face.
>
> Ther nas quyksilver, litarge, ne bremstone,
> Boras, ceruce, ne oille of tartre noon,
> Ne oynement that wold clense and byte,
> That him might helpen of his *whelkes* white,
> Ne of the *knobbes* sittyng on his cheekes."

101. *We give express charge*, etc. See Holinshed, p. 138 above.

104. *Lenity.* The folio has "Leuitie ;" an obvious misprint.

107. *Habit.* The herald's coat. The person of a herald being inviolable, he was distinguished by a peculiar dress.

108. *Of thee* From thee. Gr. 166.

108. *A fool's bolt.* A *bolt* was a blunt-headed arrow.

118. *Peevish.* Silly, childish; its ordinary if not its only meaning in S. Cf. *Rich. III.* i. 3. 194, iii. 1. 31, iv. 2. 100, etc. Steevens (in his note on *Cymb.* i. 6. 54) gives many examples of this sense from other old writers. Schmidt does not recognize the modern meaning in his *Lexicon;* Wb., strangely enough, makes no reference to this obsolete one.

119. *Fat-brained.* Dull, stupid.

121. *Apprehension.* Capacity to apprehend, perception, intelligence. Cf. *Ham.* ii. 2. 319 : "in apprehension how like a God!"

132. *Robustious.* Stout, sturdy. Cf. *Ham.* iii. 2. 10 : "a robustious periwig-pated fellow." *Robust* does not occur in S.

133. *Give them,* etc. Boswell quotes Otway, *Venice Preserved:*

> "Give but an Englishman . . .
> Beef, and a sea-coal fire, he's yours for ever."

PROLOGUE.—2. *Poring.* "That is, straining its eyes and yet seeing only the nearest things, purblind" (Schmidt).

3. *Fills.* For the form, see Gr. 336.

5. *Stilly.* Softly. Used nowhere else by S. Cf. *M. N. D.* iv. 1. 80 (stage-direction), and see note in our ed. p. 174. St. quotes from an account of the baptism of Prince Frederick Henry, 1594 : "After which ensued a still noyse of recorders and flutes."

6. *That.* So that. Gr. 283. According to Holinshed, the armies were only two hundred and fifty paces from each other.

9. *Battle.* Army ; as in iv. 2. 54 below. Cf. *K. John,* iv. ii. 78 : "two dreadful battles set," etc. In iv. 3. 69 below, *battles* = battalions ; as in *J. C.* v. 1. 4, etc.

Umber'd. Schmidt explains this as "embrowned, darkened;" but it seems better to understand it as referring to the effect of the fire-light on their faces. Malone remarks that umber, "mixed with water, produces such a dusky yellow colour as the gleam of fire by night gives to the countenance." Taken in this sense, it is an exceedingly *picturesque* word.

11. *The night's dull ear.* Steevens quotes Milton, *L'All.* 42 : "And singing startle the dull night."

12. *Accomplishing.* Furnishing, making complete. According to Douce, *closing rivets up* refers to fastening the bottom of the casque to the top of the cuirass, which was done after both had been put on.

16. *Name.* The folio has "nam'd," which was corrected by Tyrwhitt.

18, 19. Cf. Holinshed's statement that "the soldiers the night before had plaid the Englishmen at dice" (p. 139 above).

Over-lusty="too lively and merry" (Schmidt). Cf. *Lear,* ii. 4. 10: "over-lusty at legs."

20. *Cripple tardy-gaited.* The folio gives it "creeple-tardy-gated."

26. *Investing.* Attending (Schmidt). Warb. would read "invest in," that is, clothed in ; and Heath, "in fasting."

27. *Presenteth.* Steevens's emendation of the "Presented" of the folio.

28. *Who.* The relative, not the interrogative, referring to *him* in 31. Gr. 251.

35. *No note.* Nothing to indicate. Cf. *Much Ado,* iii. 2. 54: "The greatest note of it is his melancholy," etc.

36. *Enrounded.* Surrounded. Gr. 440.

38. *All-watched.* "Watched throughout" (Schmidt), spent in watching. Gr. 374.

39. *Freshly looks.* Cf. *A. Y. L.* iii. 2. 243 : "Looks he as freshly," etc. *Overbears attaint*=represses the anxiety that wears upon him. H. explains it, "overcomes all disposition on the part of the soldiers to blame or reproach him for the plight he is in ;" but this does not agree so well with the context. The king puts on a cheerful look himself, and thus revives the drooping spirits of his soldiers. Cf. Virgil, *Æn.* i. 208 :

> "Talia voce refert, curisque ingentibus aeger,
> Spem vultu simulat, premit altum corde dolorem."

41. *That.* So that. See on 6 above.

43. *A largess,* etc. Holt White quotes Quinctilian, *Inst.* i. 2: "Non enim vox illa preceptoris, ut coena, minus pluribus sufficit ; sed ut sol, universis idem lucis calorisque largitur."

45. *Then, mean and gentle all,* etc. The folio has

> "Thawing cold feare, that meane and gentle all
> Behold, as may vnworthinesse define.
> A little touch of *Harry* in the Night,
> And so our Scene," etc.

We have adopted (with D. and others) the emendation of Theo., who says : "As this stood, it was a most perplex'd and nonsensical passage ; and could not be intelligible but as I have corrected it. The poet first expatiates on the real influence that Harry's eye had on his camp ; and then addressing himself to every degree of his audience, he tells them, he'll shew (as well as his unworthy pen and powers can describe it) a little touch or sketch of this hero in the night; a faint resemblance of that cheerfulness and resolution which this brave prince expressed in himself and inspired in his followers." K., W., and the Camb. editors retain the folio reading, with some changes in pointing. They understand *mean and gentle* to refer to the various ranks of the English army. *That* must then be =*so that;* and *as may unworthiness define* would appear to mean, so far as inferior natures can appreciate it. Perhaps, as Delius conjectures, a line is lost after 45.

51. *Foils.* Swords used in fencing; here=fencers, or swordsmen.

54. *Minding.* Calling to mind, thinking of.

SCENE I.—7. *Husbandry.* Thrift, economy. Cf. *T. and C.* i. 2. 7:

"And, like as there were husbandry in war,
Before the sun rose he was harness'd light."

10. *Dress us.* Prepare ourselves. Cf. 1 *Hen. IV.* iii. 2. 51: "And dress'd myself in such humility," etc. Some eds. print it "'dress," as if a contraction of *address;* but the original meaning of *dress* is to put in order, prepare. See Wb.

16. *Likes me.* Pleases me, suits me. See on iii. prol. 32; and cf. iv. 3. 77.

19. *Upon example.* "Through comparing them with what others endure" (J. H.).

23. *Casted.* Cast off. Cf. *T. N.* ii. 5. 161: "cast thy humble slough." S. elsewhere uses *cast* for the participle; as in *A. Y. L.* iii. 4. 16, etc. *Slough*=the skin of a snake; as in the passage from *T. N.* just quoted. See also 2 *Hen. VI.* iii. 1. 229. *Legerity*=lightness, alacrity; used by S. only here.

26. *Do my good morrow.* Cf. *J. C.* iv. 2. 5: "To do you salutation," etc. Gr. 303.

27. *Desire.* Invite. Cf. *T. of C.* iv. 5. 150:

"I would desire
My famous cousin to our Grecian tents."

28, 29. For the measure, see Gr. 513.

32. *I would.* On *would*=wish, see Gr. 329.

34. *God-a-mercy.* A corruption of "God have mercy;" here, as often =gramercy, thank you (Schmidt). Cf. *K. John,* i. 1. 185; *Ham.* ii. 2. 172, etc.

38. *Popular.* Of the people, plebeian. Cf. *Cor.* ii. 1. 230, ii. 3. 109, iii. 1. 106, etc.

39. *Gentleman.* On the measure here and in 42, see Gr. 465.

40. *Trail'st thou,* etc. Farmer quotes Chapman, *Revenge for Honour:* "Fit for the trayler of the puissant pike."

44. *Bawcock.* See on iii. 2. 22.

45. *Imp.* Youngling. Used only by Armado, Holofernes, and Pistol. Cf. *L. L. L.* i. 2. 5, v. 2. 592, and 2 *Hen. IV.* v. 5. 46. Steevens quotes Holinshed: "his sonne prince Edward, that goodlie impe."

On the measure of the line, see Gr. 505.

60. *The figo.* See on iii. 6. 54 above.

63. *Sorts.* Agrees. Cf. *M. N. D.* v. 1. 55 : "not sorting with a nuptial ceremony," etc.

65. *Lower.* The quarto of 1600 has "lewer," changed to "lower" in that of 1608 ; the folio has "fewer," which Steevens was inclined to favour as a provincialism=lower. He adds : "In Sussex I heard one female servant say to another : Speak fewer, or my mistress will hear you."

85. *I think it be.* Cf. *C. of E.* v. 1. 379 : "I think it be, sir," etc. Gr. 299.

91. *Thomas.* The folio has "John."

99. *Element.* Sky. Cf. *2 Hen. IV.* iv. 3. 58. See also *J. C.* i. 3. 128, and note in our ed. p. 140. *Shows*=appears, looks. Cf. ii. 2. 127 above.

101. *Conditions.* Qualities. Cf. *Much Ado,* iii. 2. 68 : "his ill conditions," etc.

105. *Be.* See Gr. 300.

106. *Possess him,* etc. Cf. 275 below : "Possess them not with fear ;" 1 *Hen. IV.* ii. 2. 112 : "possessed with fear," etc.

110. *As cold a night as 't is.* See Gr. 276.

113. *My conscience.* My judgment, my opinion. Cf. *2 Hen. VI.* iii. 1. 68 : "Shall I speak my conscience ?"

117. *A many.* See on iii. 7. 61 ; and cf. iv. 3. 95 below.

118. *To wish him.* As to wish him. Gr. 281.

121. *Quarrel.* Often = cause or motive of quarrel (Schmidt). Cf. *Macb.* iv. 3. 137, and see note in our ed. p. 153.

131. *Latter.* Last ; as often. Cf. 1 *Hen. IV.* v. 1. 92 ; 1 *Hen. VI.* ii. 5. 38 ; *A. and C.* iv. 6. 39, etc.

134. *Rawly.* "Without due preparation and provision" (Schmidt). Cf. *rawness* in *Macb.* iv. 3. 26.

Afeard. Used by S. interchangeably with *afraid.* Cf. *M. N. D.* iii. 1. 28 ; *Macb.* i. 7. 39, etc.

136. *When blood is their argument.* When engaged in "bloody business" (*Macb.* ii. 1. 48, *Oth.* iii. 3. 469). See on iii. 1. 21 above.

138. *Who to disobey.* See Gr. 274.

139. *All proportion of subjection.* All "reasonable service."

141. *Miscarry upon the sea.* Be lost at sea. Cf. *M. for M.* iii. 1. 217 : "who miscarried at sea ;" *M. of V.* ii. 8. 29 : "there miscarried a vessel of our country," etc.

151. *Never so.* See Gr. 52, 406.

154. *Contrived murther.* Plotted, preconcerted murder. Cf. *Oth.* i. 2. 3 : "To do no contrived murther."

158. *Native.* In their own country. Cf. iv. 3. 96 below : "native graves."

161. *Before-breach.* See Gr. 429.

166. *The which.* See Gr. 270.

169. *Dying so.* For the participle, see Gr. 378.

175. *Man.* For the "confusion of construction," see Gr. 417.

187. *An elder gun.* A pop-gun.

188. *Go about.* Attempt, undertake. Cf. *M. N. D.* iv. 1. 212 ; *Much Ado,* i. 3. 12, iv. 1. 65, iv. 2. 28, etc.

189. *With.* By. Gr. 193.

191. *Round.* Plain-spoken, blunt. Cf. *T. N.* ii. 3. 102: "I must be round with you;" *Lear,* i. 4. 58: "he answered me in the roundest manner," etc.

203. *Take thee a box on the ear.* Cf. iv. 7. 118 below; also *M. for M.* ii. 1. 189, *T. of S.* iii. 2. 165, *T. N.* ii. 5. 75, etc.

211. *French crowns.* A *French crown* was a common expression for a bald head (cf. *M. for M.* i. 2. 52; *M. N. D.* i. 2. 99; *A. W.* ii. 2. 23, etc.); but the pun here, as Tyrwhitt remarks, may turn simply on the double meaning of *crown.* To cut French crowns is an allusion to the crime of clipping coin.

216. *Careful.* Full of care, anxious. Cf. *Rich. II.* ii. 2. 75: "careful business;" *C. of E.* v. 1. 298: "careful hours," etc.

220. *Wringing.* Suffering. Cf. *Much Ado,* v. 1. 28: "To those that wring under the load of sorrow."

230. *Thy soul of adoration.* The soul of thy adoration, the essential nature which men adore in thee. The folio reads: "What? is thy soul of odoration?" Johnson wished to read, "What is thy soul, O adoration?"—that is, "O reverence paid to kings, what art thou within? What are thy real qualities? What is thy intrinsic value?" Malone reads, "What is the soul," etc.

245. *Balm.* The anointing-oil used in the coronation ceremony. Cf. *Rich. II.* iii. 2. 55, iv. 1. 207; *2 Hen. IV.* iv. 5. 115. See also *Hen. VIII.* iv. 1. 88. On *ball,* cf. *Macb.* iv. 1. 121.

248. *The farced title,* etc. "The extended or swollen title prefixed to *the king,* as for example *His Most Gracious Majesty,* the king" (J. H.). For *fore,* see on ii. 2. 1 above.

255. *Distressful.* Earned by painful labour.

260. *Helps Hyperion to his horse.* Is up before the sun.

265. *Had the forehand,* etc. Would have the advantage of a king.

267. *Wots.* Knows. Used only in the present tense and the participle *wotting.* Cf. *M. N. D.* iv. 1. 161, etc. *Wots what watch* would hardly be tolerated by modern rhetoric.

269. *The peasant best advantages.* Most benefit the peasant. For the verb, cf. *Temp.* i. 1. 34: "our own doth little advantage." See also *V. and A.* 950; *J. C.* iii. 1. 242, etc. For the form, see Gr. 412, and cf. 333.

273. *Shall do't.* Will do it. Gr. 315.

276. *If.* The folio has "of;" the emendation is Tyrwhitt's. Theo. had suggested "lest." K. and Sr. point the passage thus:

> "Take from them now
> The sense of reckoning of the opposed numbers!
> Pluck their hearts from them not to-day, O Lord,
> O not to-day! Think not upon the fault," etc.

The Camb. editors suggest that a line may have been lost, which with the help of the quarto they supply as follows:

> "Take from them now
> The sense of reckoning of the opposed numbers,
> Lest that the multitudes which stand before them
> Pluck their hearts from them."

279. *Compassing.* Obtaining. Cf. *T. G. of V.* ii. 4. 214 : "to compass her I 'll use my skill," etc.

286. *Chantries.* "One of these monasteries was for Carthusian monks, and was called *Bethlehem ;* the other was for religious men and women of the order of Saint Bridget, and was named *Sion.* They were on opposite sides of the Thames, and adjoined the royal manor of Sheen, now called Richmond" (Malone).

287. *Still.* Continually. Gr. 69.

288–290. Johnson explains the passage thus : "I do all this, says the King, though all that I can do is nothing worth, is so far from an adequate expiation of the crime, that penitence comes after all, imploring pardon both for the crime and the expiation." Heath's explanation is perhaps to be preferred : "I am sensible that everything of this kind (works of piety and charity) which I have done or can do, will avail nothing towards the remission of this sin ; since I well know that, after all this is done, true repentance, and imploring pardon, are previously and indispensably necessary towards my obtaining it."

SCENE II.—4. *Via*, etc. Begone "the dull elements of earth and water !" Cf. iii. 7. 20 above, and see note on the passage.

5. *Rien puis ? l'air*, etc. "Can you add nothing more ? Is he not air and fire ? Yes, says the Dauphin, and even heaven itself" (Malone).

11. *Dout.* Do out, put out. Cf. *Ham.* iv. 7. 192 : "this folly douts," etc. The folio in both passages has "doubt," which W. retains here, making it =to make to doubt, to terrify ; a sense not found elsewhere in S.

14. *Embattled.* In battle array. Cf. *K. John*, iv. 2. 200 : "embattled and ranked," etc. It is used intransitively in *A. and C.* iv. 1. 93 :

"and they say we shall embattle
By the second hour i' the morn."

17. *Suck away their souls.* Steevens quotes Dryden, *Don Sebastian:* "Sucking each other's souls while we expire," and Pope, *Eloisa to Abelard:* "Suck my last breath, and catch my flying soul."

18. *Shales.* Shells. Used by S. nowhere else.

21. *Curtle-axe.* Cutlass (Schmidt). Cf. *A. Y. L.* i. 3. 119 : "A gallant curtle-axe upon my thigh."

28. *Squares.* Squadrons. Cf. *A. and C.* iii. 11. 40 : "the brave squares of war."

29. *Hilding.* Properly a noun =a base menial. Cf. *T. of S.* ii. 1. 26 : "For shame, thou hilding," etc. It is used again as an adjective in 2 *Hen. IV.* i. 1. 57 : "He was some hilding fellow."

31. *Idle speculation.* Inactive looking-on.

32. *What 's to say ?* Cf. *T. N.* iii. 3. 18 : "What 's to do ?" Gr. 359.

35. *Tucket sonance.* A *tucket* was a flourish on a trumpet. Steevens quotes *The Spanish Tragedy :* "a tucket afar off." *Sonance* = sound. Cf. Heywood, *Rape of Lucrece*, 1630 : "to hear their sonance."

36. *Dare the field.* "He uses terms of the field as if they were going out only to the chase for sport. To *dare the field* is a phrase in falconry. Birds are dared when by the falcon in the air they are terrified from

rising, so that they will be sometimes taken by the hand. Such an easy capture the lords expected to make of the English" (Johnson). Cf. *Hen. VIII.* iii. 2. 282 : "dare us with his cap like larks."

39. *Desperate of their bones.* Cf. *Oth.* ii. 3. 337 : "I am desperate of my fortunes."

41. *Their ragged curtains.* Their tattered banners.

44. *Beaver.* The visor of a helmet. Cf. *2 Hen. IV.* iv. 1. 120 : "their beavers down ;" *Ham.* i. 2. 230 : "he wore his beaver up."

45. *Like fixed candlesticks.* "Grandpré alludes to the form of ancient candlesticks, which frequently represented human figures holding the sockets for the lights in their extended hands" (Steevens). Cf. *Vittoria Corombona,* 1612 : "he showed like a pewter candlestick, fashioned like a man in armour, holding a tilting staff in his hand little bigger than a candle."

47. *Lob down.* Hang down, droop.

51. *Gimmal bit.* A bit made of rings or links. Steevens cites *King Edward III.* i. 2 : "Nor lay aside their jacks of gymold mail." *Gim-maled mail* was armour composed of links like those of a chain. Malone quotes Minsheu, *Dict.,* 1619 : "A gimmal or gemmow from the Gal. *gemeau,* Lat. *gemellus,* double, or twinnes, because they be rings with two or more links."

60. *Guidon.* The folio has "guard ; on," etc. The emendation is found in Rann's ed., and is adopted by the Camb. editors, K., and others. It is favoured by what follows ; but the folio reading is defended by Ma-lone, who considers that "*guard* means here nothing more than the *men of war* whose duty it was to attend on the Constable of France, and among those his *standard,* that is, his standard-bearer."

62. *For.* Because of. Gr. 150.

63. *Outwear.* Are wearing away, wasting. Cf. *V. and A.* 841 : "Her song was tedious and outwore the night ;" *L. L. L.* ii. 1. 23 : "Till pain-ful study shall outwear three years," etc. S. uses the word only of the lapse of time.

Scene III.—2. *Is rode.* See Gr. 295, 343.

9. For the measure, see Gr. 469.

13. *Mind.* Remind. Cf. 84 below.

15. *As full of valour,* etc. Cf. *Rich. II.* v. 5. 114 : "As full of valour as of royal blood."

16. *O that we now,* etc. Cf. extract from Holinshed, p. 139 above.

18. *What 's he,* etc. Gr. 254. For the measure, see Gr. 500.

20. *Enow.* The old plural of *enough.*

21. *To do our country loss.* Cf. *T. of S.* v. 2. 179 : "do him ease ;" *T. N.* v. 1. 136 : "to do you rest ;" *R. of L.* 597 : "to do him shame," etc.

24. *By Jove.* "The king prays like a Christian, and swears like a heathen" (Johnson).

26. *It yearns.* It grieves. Cf. *M. W.* iii. 5. 45 : "it would yearn your heart to see it." We have had the word used intransitively in ii. 3. 3, 6 above.

M

35. *That he,* etc.   For the "confusion of construction," see Gr. 415.

37. *Convoy.*   Travelling expenses.

40. *The feast of Crispian.*   The 25th of October, Saint Crispin's day. Crispin and Crispian were brothers, born in Rome ; whence they travelled to Soissons, France, about A.D. 303, to propagate the Christian religion.   They supported themselves by working at their trade of shoemaking ; but the governor of the town, learning that they were Christians, caused them to be beheaded.   They subsequently became the tutelar saints of the shoemakers.

41. The folio reads : " He that shall see this day, and liue old age." The transposition was made by Pope, and is favoured by the quarto reading, " He that outlives this day and sees old age."

45. *The vigil.*   The evening before the festival.

48. This line, omitted in the folio, is restored from the quarto.

50. *With advantages. Advantage* sometimes means interest upon money ; as in *M. of V.* i. 3. 71, 1 *Hen. IV.* ii. 4. 599.   Here it is used metaphorically in the same sense ; as in *K. John,* iii. 3. 22 : " And with advantage means to pay thy love."

63. *Gentle his condition.*   "Advance him to the rank of a gentleman" (Johnson).   On *gentle,* see Gr. 290.

68. *Bestow yourself.*   " Repair to your post " (Schmidt).

69. *Bravely.*   With great display.   Cf. *Temp.* v. i. 224 : " bravely rigged," etc.   *Battles*=battalions.   See on iv. prol. 9 above.

70. *Expedience.*   Expedition, haste.   Cf. *Rich. II.* ii. 1. 287 : " making hither with all due expedience."   So *expediently*=quickly in *A. Y. L.* iii. 1. 18 : " Do this expediently," etc.

77. *Likes me.*   Pleases me.   See on iv. 1. 16 above.   Gr. 297.

83. *Englutted.*   Swallowed up.   Cf. *Oth.* i. 3. 57 : " it engluts and swallows other sorrows ;" *T. of A.* ii. 2 175 :

> " How many prodigal bits have slaves and peasants
>   This night englutted !"

84. On *thee,* see Gr. 414 ; and on *wilt mind,* Gr. 348.   See also on 13 above.

86. *Retire.*   See Gr. 451.

91. *Achieve.*   " Finish, kill " (Schmidt).   Some make it=capture, get possession of ; as in *M. of V.* iii. 2. 210, etc.

94. *With.*   See Gr. 193.

95. *A many.*   See on iii. 7. 61 above.

104. *Abounding.*   Theo. preferred to read "a bounding," which some eds. adopt.

107. *Relapse.*   For the accent, see Gr. 492.

109. *For the working-day.*   Cf. i. 2. 277 above.

110. *Gilt.*   Gilding.   Cf. *T. of A.* iv. 3. 302 : " in thy gilt and thy perfume ;" *Rich. II.* ii. 1. 294 : " our sceptre's gilt," etc.   W. misprints " guilt."

114. *Slovenry.*   Slovenliness ; used by S. nowhere else.

117. *Or they will pluck,* etc.   Though they have to pluck, etc.

130. *Vaward.*   Vanguard.   Cf. *Cor.* i. 6. 53 : " Their bands i' the va

ward," etc. It is used metaphorically in *M. N. D.* iv. 1. 110 and 2 *Hen. IV.* i. 2. 199.

132. *How.* As. Gr. 46.

SCENE IV.—4. *Callino*, etc. The folio has "Qualtitie calmie custure me." Various emendations had been proposed before Boswell found an old Irish song called "Callino, castore me," which, he suggests, Pistol probably hums contemptuously. .

9. *Fox.* A cant word for *sword*. The figure of a fox was often engraved on blades. Steevens quotes B. and F., *Philaster:* "I made my father's old fox fly about his ears;" and *The Two Angry Women of Abington*, 1599 : "I had a sword, ay the flower of Smithfield for a sword ; a right fox, i' faith."

15. *Rim.* Steevens remarks that some part of the intestines was anciently called the *rim*, and quotes Sir Arthur Gorges, *Lucan*, 1614 :

> "The slender rimme too weake to part
> The boyling liver from the heart."

The word is also used by Holland in his *Pliny*, and by Chapman in his *Iliad*. Cole, in his *Dict.*, 1678, describes it as the caul in which the bowels are wrapped.

19. *Brass.* As Sir W. Rawlinson notes, either S. had little knowledge of French or his fondness for punning led him here into an error ; for the *s* in *bras* is silent. Johnson suggested that the pronunciation may have been different in the time of S., but Malone and Douce have proved that it was the same as now. Sir W. Davenant makes the word rhyme with *draw ;* and Eliot, in his *Orthoepia Gallica*, 1593, directs that *bras de fer* be pronounced "bra de fer." K. thinks that though the Frenchman might have said *bra*, the sound might have suggested to Pistol the word which he had seen written *bras ;* but this seems a little forced.

20. *Luxurious.* Lustful ; as always in S. Cf. *luxury* in iii. 5. 6.

23. *Moys.* Apparently meant for money of some kind, and perhaps suggested by *moidore*, though Johnson is wrong in giving the derivation of that word as "*moi d'or.*" Douce says that *moy* was a measure of corn, but it is not likely that it has that meaning here.

24. *Ask me.* For the omission of the preposition, see Gr. 201.

29. *Firk.* Beat, drub (Schmidt). *Ferret* = worry, as a ferret does its game. Schmidt quotes the old play of *King Leir:* "I 'll ferret you ere night for that word."

70. *This roaring devil*, etc. In the old "moralities" or comedies, the Vice or buffoon had a sword or dagger of lath with which he used to beat the devil, and sometimes attempted to pare his long nails. Cf. *T. N.* iv. ii. 134 :

> "Like to the old Vice,
> . . . . .
> Who, with dagger of lath,
> In his rage and his wrath,
>   Cries, ah, ha! to the devil:
> Like a mad lad,
> Pare thy nails, dad," etc.

73. *Adventurously.* Daringly, boldly.

SCENE V.—1. Here, as in iii. 7 above, the quarto omits the Dauphin from the list of speakers. The stage-direction is simply "*Enter the foure French Lords*"—that is, "Burbon, Constable, Orleance, and Gebon" (see on iii. 7. 1).

7. *Perdurable.* Lasting. Cf. *Oth.* i. 3. 343 : "cables of perdurable toughness."

8. *Be.* Often so used in questions. Gr. 299.

11. *Let us die in honour.* The folio has "Let vs dye in once more backe againe." K. suggested the reading in the text. The quarto has "Lets dye with honour, our shame doth last too long."

12. *Friend.* Befriend. Gr. 290.

15. *On heaps.* Cf. v. 2. 39 below; also *T. and C.* iii. 2. 29, *J. C.* i. 3. 23, etc.

SCENE VI.—8. *Larding.* Enriching (Schmidt). Cf. 1 *Hen. IV.* ii. 2. 116 : "lards the lean earth," etc. The Coll. MS. substitutes "loading."

9. *Honour-owing.* Honour-owning, honourable. Cf. *Temp.* iii. 1. 45 : "the noblest grace she owed," etc.

11. *Haggled.* Cut, mangled.

12. *Insteep'd.* See Gr. 440.

18. *Well-foughten.* See Gr. 344.

21. *Raught.* The old imperfect of *reach*, and the only one in S. Cf. *L. L. L.* iv. 2. 41 ; 3 *Hen. VI.* i. 4. 68, etc. We have the participle *raught* in 2 *Hen. VI.* ii. 3. 43 and *A. and C.* iv. 9. 30 ; but *reached* in *Oth.* i. 2. 24.

22. *Dear my lord.* See Gr. 13.

24. *So.* Then. See Gr. 66.

33. *Perforce.* Necessarily ; in this sense always joined with *must.* Cf. *M. N. D.* iii. 2. 90, etc.

34. *Mistful.* The folio has "mixtful ;" the emendation is due to Warb. Some eds. read "wistful."

35. The alarum was sounded by affrighted fugitives from the English camp, who declared that the French were making an attack in the rear. Henry, not knowing the extent of the danger, gave the order for killing the prisoners (Malone).

SCENE VII.—1. *Kill the poys*, etc. The English baggage was guarded only by boys and lackeys, and some French runaways, learning this fact, attacked them and plundered the baggage. It is this villainy to which Fluellen alludes.

8. *The king most worthily*, etc. Johnson points out that the king gives one reason for killing the prisoners (iv. 6. 36), and Gower another ; but S. follows Holinshed, who gives both these reasons for Henry's conduct.

49. *I was not angry.* For the tense, see Gr. 347.

55. *Skirr.* "Move rapidly, scour" (Schmidt). Cf. *Macb.* v. 3. 35 : "skirr the country round."

56. *Enforced.* Thrown with force. Cf. 2 *Hen. IV.* iv. 1. 71, etc.

64. *Fin'd.* Fixed as the sum to be paid (Schmidt).

67. *To look.* To look for. Gr. 200. Cf. *M. W.* iv. 2. 79 : "I will look some linen ;" *A. W.* iii. 6. 115 : "I must go look my twigs," etc. The

folio has "book" in the present passage; the emendation is from the Coll. MS. K. and St. retain "book."

69. *Woe the while.* Cf. *W. T.* iii. 2. 173, and *J. C.* i. 3. 83.

74. *Yerk.* Jerk, thrust. Cf. *Oth.* i. 2. 5 : "to have yerk'd him here under the ribs."

79. *A many.* See on iii. 7. 61.

92. *In a garden,* etc. King Arthur won a great victory over the Saxons "in a garden where leeks did grow," and Saint David ordered that every one of the king's soldiers should wear a leek in his cap in honour thereof. Hence the Welsh custom of wearing the emblem on St. David's day, March 1st.

93. *Monmouth caps.* Fuller, in his *Worthies of Wales,* says : "The best caps were formerly made at Monmouth, where the Capper's chapel doth still remain." Reed quotes the old ballad of *The Caps :* "The soldiers that the Monmouth wear," etc.

108. *Our heralds go,* etc. For the construction of *go,* see Gr. 364.

109. *Just notice.* Exact information. Cf. *M. of V.* iv. 1. 327 : "a just pound ;" *Oth.* i. 3. 5 : "a just account," etc.

116. *Swaggered with me.* Bullied me. Cf. *2 Hen. IV.* ii. 4. 107 : "he 'll not swagger with a Barbary hen, if her feathers turn back in any show of resistance." On *who,* see Gr. 249.

126. *Great sort.* High rank. Cf. iv. 8. 71 below : "prisoners of good sort," etc.

Quite from the answer, etc. "Quite debarred by the laws of the duello from answering the challenge of one of such inferior rank" (J. H.). On *from* = away from, cf. *J. C.* ii. 1. 196 : "Quite from the main opinion," etc. Gr. 158. There is a play upon this sense of *from* in *Rich. III.* iv. 4. 258 : "That thou dost love my daughter from thy soul," etc.

130. *Jack-sauce.* Fluellen's blunder for *Saucy Jack.* For *Jack* as a term of contempt, cf. *1 Hen. IV.* iii. 3. 99, v. 4. 143 ; *R. and J.* ii. 4. 160 ; *M. of V.* iii. 4. 77, etc.

144. *When Alençon and myself,* etc. This alludes to an historical fact. Henry was felled to the ground by the Duke of Alençon, but recovered himself and slew two of the Duke's attendants.

165. *If that.* See Gr. 287 (cf. v. prol. 17 below) ; and for *as,* Gr. 111.

168. *Valiant.* Metrically a trisyllable. Gr. 479.

169. *Touch'd.* See Gr. 377.

170. *Will return.* For the ellipsis of the nominative, see Gr. 399.

SCENE VIII.—7. *'Sblood.* A common oath, abbreviated from *God's blood ;* usually omitted or replaced by other words in the folio (Schmidt).

20. *In a summer's day.* See on iii. 6. 61 above.

39. *Bitter terms.* Bitter words. Cf. v. 2. 99 below.

48. *Lowliness.* Humble bearing. Cf. *L. L. L.* iv. 1. 81 : "thou the beggar ; for so witnesseth thy lowliness."

56. *Needs.* Of necessity. Gr. 25.

64. *I will none,* etc. See Gr. 53.

70. *Sort.* Rank. See on iv. 7. 126 above.

84. *Mercenaries.* Hired soldiers, common soldiers.

100. *Davy Gam, esquire.* This gentleman, being sent by Henry, before the battle, to find out the strength of the enemy, made this report : " May it please you, my liege, there are enough to be killed, enough to be taken prisoners, and enough to run away." He saved the king's life in the field (Malone).

101. *Of name.* Of eminence. Cf. *Rich. II.* ii. 3. 56 : " None else of name and noble estimate."

106. *So great and little loss*, etc. Cf. *Macb.* i. 3. 60 :

> " Speak then to me, who neither beg nor fear
> Your favours nor your hate ;"

and see note in our ed. p. 162.

109. *Go we.* Cf. 118 below : " Do we all holy rites," etc. Gr. 364.

121. *We 'll.* The quarto reading, adopted by Capell, D., and others ; the folio has " And."

ACT V

PROLOGUE.—2. *Of.* From. Gr. 166.

3. *Them.* For the " redundant object," see Gr. 414.

7. For the measure, see Gr. 480.

10. *Pales in.* Encloses, encompasses. Cf. *Cymb.* iii. 1. 19 :

> " As Neptune's park, ribbed and paled in
> With rocks unscalable and roaring waters."

12. *Whiffler.* " An officer who walks first in processions, or before persons in high stations, on occasions of ceremony " (Hanmer). In the play of *Clyomon*, 1599, a whiffler makes his appearance at a tournament, clearing the way before the king. Cf. *The Isle of Gulls*, 1606 : " And Manasses shall go before like a whiffler, and make way with his horns."

17. *Where that*, etc. Where his lords wish him to have his bruised helmet, etc., borne before him. See Holinshed, p. 141 above.

21. *Giving full trophy*, etc. " Transferring all the honours of conquest, all trophies, tokens, and shows, from himself to God " (Johnson). For *quite from*, see on iv. 7. 126 above.

25. *Sort.* Manner, style. Cf. *T. of S.* iii. 1. 67 : " in a more fairer sort," etc.

26. *Antique.* Spelt *antick* or *antique* in the old eds. without regard to the meaning, but always accented on the first syllable. Gr. 492.

29. *Likelihood.* Similitude.

30. *The general.* The Earl of Essex. See Introduction, p. 10.

32. *Broached.* Spitted, transfixed. Cf. *T. A.* iv. 2. 85: "I 'll broach the tadpole on my rapier's point."

34. *Much more cause. With* may be understood, or "and *there was* much more cause" may be a parenthesis (Gr. 202).

38. *The emperor.* The folio has "emperor's ;" the emendation is M. Mason's. The reference is to the emperor Sigismond, who was married to Henry's second cousin.

41. *Back-return.* See Gr. 429, and cf. iv. 1. 161 above.

43. *Remembering you.* Reminding you. Cf. *Temp.* i. 2. 243: "Let me remember thee what thou hast promis'd," etc.

SCENE I.—5. *Scald.* Scurvy, scabby. Cf. *A. and C.* v. 2. 215: "scald rhymers ;" *M. W.* iii. 1. 123: "This same scall [Evans's pronunciation of the word], scurvy, cogging companion."

18. *Parca's fatal web.* The *Parcæ* were the Fates.

25. *Cadwallader.* The last of the Welsh kings.

27. *As eat it.* For the ellipsis, see Gr. 353.

35. *Astonished.* Johnson and Steevens explain this as=stunned (with the blow) ; M. Mason and Schmidt as=confounded, amazed. K. says that the word is still a pugilistic term=stunned.

66. *Gleeking.* Scoffing, sneering. Cf. *M. N. D.* iii. 1. 150: "I can gleek upon occasion." *Galling,* which has much the same meaning, is not elsewhere used intransitively by S.

70. *Condition.* Temper, disposition. Cf. *M. of V.* i. 2. 143: "the condition of a saint, and the complexion of a devil," etc.

72. *Huswife.* The usual spelling of *housewife* in the folio (Schmidt). The word is here used contemptuously=hussy. Cf. *A. and C.* iv. 15. 44: "the false housewife Fortune."

73. *Spital.* Hospital. Cf. ii. 1. 71 above. So *spital-house* in *T. of A.* iv. 3. 39.

77. *Cudgell'd.* The folio, which prints the passage as prose, has "Cudgeld" and " Ile turne." The quarto reads, " Bawd will I turne, and vse the slyte of hand," etc. Coll. and the Camb. ed. have "cudgelled" and "I 'll turn ;" W. has "cudgell'd" and "I 'll ;" D., K., H., and others give the reading we have adopted.

81. Johnson remarks here : "The comick scenes of The History of Henry the Fourth and Fifth are now at an end, and all the comick personages are now dismissed. Falstaff and Mrs. Quickly are dead ; Nym and Bardolph are hanged ; Gadshill was lost immediately after the robbery ; Poins and Peto have vanished since, one knows not how ; and Pistol is now beaten into obscurity. I believe every reader regrets their departure."

SCENE II.—1. *Wherefore.* For which.

17. *The fatal balls.* The eyes of the basilisk were fabled to kill with a

glance. Cf. *W. T.* i. 2. 388: "Make me not sighted like the basilisk;"
Rich. III. i. 2. 151:

> "*Gloster*. Thine eyes, sweet lady, have infected mine.
> *Anne.* Would they were basilisks, to strike thee dead!"

See also *Cymb.* ii. 4. 107, etc.   J. H. remarks: "*Balls* is here used in
word-play, implying comparison between *eye-balls* and *cannon-balls*."

19. *Have.* For the "confusion of proximity," see Gr. 412.

27. *Bar.* Barrier, place of congress (Johnson). On a previous occasion, Henry with his friends had had a conference with Katherine and
her relatives in a field near Melun, where two pavilions were erected for
the royal families, and a third between them for the interview. The
Frenchmen, according to the Chronicle, "ditched, trenched, and paled
their lodgings for fear of after-clappes; but the Englishmen had their
parte of the field only *barred* and parted." Malone suggests that S. may
here have had this former meeting in his thoughts. The present conference took place in St. Peter's Church at Troyes, but the editors agree
in supposing it to occur in a palace; because, as Malone tells us, "St.
Peter's Church would not admit of the French king and queen, etc., re-
tiring, and then appearing again on the scene." See p. 142 above.

28. *Mightiness.* Plural. See Gr. 471.

31. *Congreeted.* Met in a friendly way (Schmidt).

33. *Rub.* Hinderance. See on ii. 2. 188.

34. *Why that.* See Gr. 287; and cf. 46 below.

39. *On heaps.* See on iv. 5. 13 above.

40. *It own.* Its own. Cf. *Temp.* ii. 1. 163: "it own kind;" *Ham.* v.
1. 244: "it own life," etc. See Gr. 228, or *Temp.* p. 120.

42. *Even-pleach'd.* "Interwoven so as to have a smooth and even
surface" (Schmidt). Cf. *Much Ado*, i. 2. 10: "a thick-pleach'd alley;"
Id. iii. 1. 7: "the pleached bower," etc.

45. *Fumitory.* The plant *Fumaria* (five species are found in England),
called *fumiter* in *Lear*, iv. 4. 3. For *doth* in next line, see Gr. 334.

47. *Deracinate.* Uproot, extirpate. Cf. *T. and C.* i. 3. 99:

> "rend and deracinate
> The unity and married calm of states
> Quite from their fixure!"

Savagery here = wild growth; in *K. John*, iv. 3. 48, it means savage conduct, atrocity.

49. *Freckled cowslip.* Cf. *M. N. D.* ii. 1. 10:

> "The cowslips tall her pensioners be;
> In their gold coats spots you see;
> Those be rubies, fairy favours,
> In those freckles live their savours."

The *burnet* is the *Poterium sanguisorba*. It was valued as a salad plant,
and Bacon (*Essay of Gardens*, ed. 1625) says of it: "But those which
Perfume the aire most delightfully, not *passed by* as the rest, but being
Troden upon and *Crushed*, are Three: That is Burnet, Wilde-Time, and
Water-Mints. Therefore, you are to set whole Allies of them, to have
the Pleasure when you walke or tread."

52. *Kecksies.* Properly the dried and withered ste[m]
but the name is occasionally applied to the living plan[t]

61. *Diffus'd.* The folio has "defus'd;" as in [A]
Schmidt would retain that form, explaining it as = "s[...]
defined *diffus'd* as "extravagant;" Johnson, as "wild,

63. *Favour.* Aspect, appearance. Cf. *J. C.* i. 2. 9[...]

65. *Let.* Impediment, hinderance. Cf. *R. of L.* 3[...]

68. *Would.* Wish. Gr. 329.

73. *Enschedul'd.* Written down. Gr. 440.

77. *Cursorary.* Cursory, hasty. The folio has "curselarie," the quarto "cursenary."

78. *Pleaseth.* May it please. Gr. 361.

79. *Presently.* Immediately; as in iii. 2. 49. Cf. *Temp.* i. 2. 125, iv. 1. 42, etc.

82. *Pass our accept.* Declare our acceptance. Malone conjectured "pass or accept" (=agree to, or take exception to), which is also in the Coll. MS.

84. Neither *Clarence* nor *Huntington* appear in the *dramatis personæ*, as neither speaks a word. Huntington was John Holland, Earl of Huntington, who afterwards married the widow of Edmond Mortimer, Earl of March (Malone).

88. *Advantageable.* Profitable. The Coll. MS. reads "advantage."

90. *Consign.* Agree. Cf. *2 Hen. IV.* v. 2. 143: "God consigning to my good intents," etc.

92. *Our gracious brother.* See Gr. 13.

94. *Too nicely urg'd.* Too sophistically pressed.

128. *Clap hands.* In token of betrothal. Cf. *W. T.* p. 152, note on 104.

131. *You undid me.* You would undo me.

133. *In measure.* That is, in dancing. There is a play on the different senses of the word; as in *Much Ado*, ii. 1. 74, *L. L. L.* iv. 3. 384, and *Rich. II.* iii. 4. 7.

137. *Buffet.* Box. Cf. *K. John*, ii. 1. 465:

> "Our ears are cudgell'd; not a word of his
> But buffets better than a fist of France."

138. *Jack-an-apes.* An ape or monkey. Cf. *M. W.* iv. 4. 67; *A. W.* iii. 5. 88, etc.

139. *Greenly.* Foolishly. Cf. *Ham.* iv. 5. 83: "we have done but greenly," etc. See also iv. prol. 39: "But freshly looks."

140. *Nor have I no.* See Gr. 406.

145. *I speak to thee plain soldier.* Cf. *K. John*, ii. 1. 462: "He speaks plain cannon fire;" *A. Y. L.* iii. 2. 227: "speak sad brow and true maid," etc.

149. *Plain and uncoined constancy.* That is, like a plain piece of metal, that has not yet received any impression.

Perforce. See on iv. 6. 33 above.

154. *Will fall.* Will fall away, shrink.

176. *Saint Denis.* The patron saint of France. Cf. *L. L. L.* v. 2. 87 [...] " Saint Denis to Saint Cupid!"

196. *Scambling.* Scrambling, struggling. Cf. i. 1. 4 above,

4. Très-cher et divin. The error in gender may be intentional; but
me editors print "très-chère et divine," though they do not correct
the preceding *mon.* The folio has "*trescher & deuin;*" the passage is
not found in the quartos.

210. *Untempering.* Not producing the desired effect, not moving or
persuading. Cf. *temper* = fashion, mould; as in ii. 2. 118 above. See
also *T. A.* iv. 4. 109.

228. *Broken music.* Mr. Chappell (*Popular Music of the Olden Time*,
p. 246) explained this as "the music of a stringed band;" but, according
to Mr. W. A. Wright (C. P. ed. of *A. Y. L.* p. 89), he has since altered his
opinion, and now gives the following explanation: "Some instruments,
such as viols, violins, flutes, etc., were formerly made in sets of four,
which when played together formed a 'consort.' If one or more of the
instruments of one set were substituted for the corresponding ones of
another set, the result was no longer a 'consort,' but 'broken music.'"
Cf. *T. and C.* iii. 1. 52 and *A. Y. L.* i. 2. 150, where, as here, there is a
play upon the expression. See also Bacon, *Essay* 37: "accompanied
with some broken Musicke."

240. *D'une votre indigne serviteur.* The folio has "*d'une nostre Seigneur indignie seruiteur,*" which is nonsense. The *Var.* of 1821, following
Pope, reads, "*d'une vostre indigne serviteure,*" which is adopted by K.,
W., H., and others; but we are not aware that there is any authority for
the form *serviteure.* D. prints "serviteur." The Camb. editors give a
reading of their own: "d'une de votre seigneurie indigne serviteur."

We may remark here, by the way, that we see no more reason for re-
taining the old French orthography in the text than the old English.
We follow D. in giving the modern spelling.

255. *List.* Barrier, boundary. Cf. *A. Y. L.* ii. 1. 53; 1 *Hen. IV.* iv. 1.
51; *Ham.* iv. 5. 99, etc.

257. *Find-faults.* Fault-finders. For similar compounds, see Gr. 432.

269. *Condition.* Temper, disposition. See on v. 1. 70 above. *Smooth*
= bland, gentle. Cf. 1 *Hen. IV.* i. 3. 7:

> "my condition,
> Which hath been smooth as oil, soft as young **down.**"

279. *Consign.* Agree. Cf. 90 above.

290. *This moral.* "That is, the application of this fable. The *moral*
being the application of a fable, our author calls any application a
moral" (Johnson). Cf. iii. 6. 35 above; also *Much Ado*, iii. 5. 78,
M. N. D. v. 1. 120, *T. of S.* iv. 4. 79, etc.

297. *Perspectively.* As through a *perspective;* an optical contrivance,
for which see *Rich. II.* ii. 2. 18, and note in our ed. p. 180.

299. *Maiden walls*, etc. Malone quotes *R. of L.* 468 and *L. C.* 176; to
which might be added *A. W.* i. 1. 137.

309. *According*, etc. That is, in the exact form in which they were
proposed.

315. *Præclarissimus.* It should be *præcarissimus*, as it is in the original treaty (printed in Rymer's *Fœdera*); but S. copied the error (doubtless a typographical one) from Holinshed. The fact that the poet did
not correct it confirms Ben Jonson's statement that he had "small Latin."

328. *That never war*, etc. So that war may never, etc. Gr. 368.

332. *I kiss her.* In accordance with the ancient ceremony of affiancing (J. H.). Cf. *T. N.* v. 1. 161 : "Attested by the holy close of lips;" *K. John*, ii. 1. 534 :

> "*King Philip.* It likes us well ; young princes, close your hands.
> *Austria.* And your lips too;" etc.

339. *Paction.* Agreement, alliance. The folio has "pation;" the emendation is due to Theo.

340. *Incorporate.* Cf. *M. N. D.* iii. 2. 208, etc. Gr. 342.

EPILOGUE.

1. *All-unable.* Weak, impotent. Cf. *Lear*, i. 1. 61 : "speech unable," etc.

2. *Bending.* "Unequal to the weight of his subject and bending beneath it ; or he may mean, as in *Hamlet* [iii. 2. 160], ' Here *stooping* to your clemency'" (Steevens). Schmidt is also in doubt between these two explanations, of which we are inclined to prefer the former.

4. *By starts.* That is, by a fragmentary representation.

7. *The world's best garden.* France. Cf. *T. of S.* i. 1. 4 : "The pleasant garden of great Italy." *Achiev'd*=gained, won. Cf. iv. 3. 91 above.

11. *The.* The article "frequently precedes a verbal that is followed by an object" (Gr. 93).

14. *Let this*, etc. Let this play find acceptance.

ADDENDA.

THE "TIME-ANALYSIS" OF THE PLAY.—This is summed up by Mr. P. A. Daniel (*Trans. of New Shaks. Soc.* 1877–79, p. 297) as follows :

"The period of history included in this play commences in the second year of Henry's reign, 1414, and ends with his betrothal to Katherine, 20th May, 1420.

This period is represented on the stage by nine days, with intervals.

1st CHORUS. Prologue.

Day 1. Act I. sc. i. and ii.

2d CHORUS. *Interval.*

Day 2. Act II. sc. i.

    *Interval.**

" 3. Act II. sc. ii. and iii.

    Interval. Time for the arrival of the English army in France, and for the further journey of Exeter to the French court.

---

* "Less time than one week for poor Sir John's sickness, death, and burial, cannot well be denied, and, but that kings must not be kept waiting, I should have set down at least a fortnight."

Day 4. Act II. sc. iv.
3d Chorus. *Interval.*
Day 5. Act III. sc. i.–iii.
　　　　Interval. March of King Henry towards Calais.
　　　　[Act III. sc. iv. Some time of the interval succeeding Day 4.]
" 6. Act III. sc. v.
　　　　Interval ; a day or two.
" 7. Act III. sc. vi.,* and first part of sc. vii.
" 8. Act III. sc. vii., second part. 4th Chorus, and Act IV. sc. i.–viii.
5th Chorus. *Interval.*
　　　　[Act V. sc. i. Some time in the early part of the last Interval.†]
Day 9. Act V. sc. ii.
6th Chorus. Epilogue."

Drawn (p. 154). *Drawn*=with drawn sword ; as in *Temp.* ii. 1. 308 : "Why are you drawn ?" See also *M. N. D.* iii. 2. 402, *R. and J.* i. 1. 73, etc. Gr. 374.

Of sack (p. 158). *Sack* was "the generic name of Spanish and Canary wines" (Schmidt) ; but sometimes the particular kind was specified. Cf. 2 *Hen. IV.* iv. 3. 104 : "a good Sherris-sack ;" that is, Sherry wine. Nares quotes the ballad of *Mad Tom :* "a cup of Malaga sack ;" and Herrick :

> "thy isles shall lack
> Grapes, before Herrick leaves Canarie sack."

The fatal balls (p. 183). There is also a play upon the word *basilisk*, which sometimes meant a piece of heavy ordnance. Cf. 1 *Hen. IV.* ii. 3. 56 : "Of basilisks, of cannon, culverin ;" also Marlowe, *Jew of Malta :*

> "Which with our bombards, shot, and basilisk,
> We rent in sunder at our entry," etc.

---

* "In this scene we have a noticeable instance of the method in which time is frequently dealt with in these plays ; the progress of events keeping pace with the dialogue in which they are narrated. Pistol comes to urge Fluellen to intercede with Exeter for Bardolph, who is sentenced to be hanged for stealing a pax of little price ; Fluellen declines to interfere, and almost immediately after—without his quitting the stage, and without any break in the action which might assist the spectator in imagining the passage of time—he is able to inform the King, who enters, that Bardolph's 'nose is executed, and his fire's out.' "

† "Yesterday, it seems, was St. David's Day, and Pistol, in fulfilment of his vow recorded in Act IV. sc. i., had taken advantage of Fluellen's presence in a place where he 'could not breed no contention,' to insult him about his leek. Fluellen now revenges himself, and cudgels Pistol into eating the leek he loathed. The locality of this scene is France ; for in his last speech, Pistol says, 'to England will I steal :' its time, dramatically considered, should probably be imagined within a few days of Day 8. Pistol's braggardism had been pretty thoroughly exposed to the world already, and he could scarcely be expected to maintain the imposture for any longer time. Johnson, it may be observed, would place the scene at the end of Act IV., supposing it to occur before the return of the army to England. At a pinch, perhaps, we might imagine that Pistol, with Fluellen and Gower, had remained in garrison at Calais since the great battle, and, if we go by the Almanac, we might thus lengthen out Pistol's military career by four months and a half to this 2d March, the morrow of St. David's Day. This time and place, too, might be taken to agree pretty well with the news that Pistol has received from England that his 'Nell is dead i' the spital ;' but it seems idle to assign any definite position in our time-plot to this scene, and I enclose it therefore within brackets ; referring it to some time in the early part of the interval marked by Chorus 5."

LIST OF CHARACTERS IN THE PLAY, WITH THE SCENES IN WHICH THEY APPEAR. — The numbers in parentheses indicate the lines the characters have in each scene.

King Henry: i. 2(120) ; ii. 2(137) ; iii. 1(34), 3(51), 6(45) ; iv. 1(213), 3(95), 6(12), 7(65), 8(58) ; v. 2(233). Whole no. 1063.

Gloucester: iii. 6(1) ; iv. 1(2), 3(1), 7(1). Whole no. 5.

Bedford: i. 2(3) ; iv. 3(4). Whole no. 7.

Exeter: i. 2(16) ; ii. 2(11), 4(57) , iv. 3(4), 6(27), 7(2), 8(5) ; v. 2(8). Whole no. 130.

York: iv. 3(2). Whole no. 2.

Salisbury: iii. 3(9). Whole no. 9.

Westmoreland: i. 2(14) ; ii. 2(3) ; iv. 3(7) ; v. 2(3). Whole no. 27.

Warwick: iv. 8(1). Whole no. 1.

Canterbury: i. 1(82), 2(141). Whole no. 223.

Ely: i. 1(20), 2(7). Whole no. 27.

Cambridge: ii. 2(15). Whole no. 15.

Scroop: ii. 2(13). Whole no. 13.

Grey : ii. 2(13). Whole no. 13.

Erpingham: iv. 1(7). Whole no. 7.

Gower: iii. 2(14), 6(23) ; iv. 1(4), 7(15), 8(1) ; v. 1(18). Whole no. 75.

Fluellen: iii. 2(48), 6(66) ; iv. 1(17), 7(83), 8(43) ; v. 1(53). Whole no. 310.

Macmorris: iii. 2(24). Whole no. 24.

Jamy: iii. 2(12). Whole no. 12.

Bates: iv. 1(21). Whole no. 21.

Court: iv. 1(2). Whole no. 2.

Williams: iv. 1(46), 7(12), 8(23). Whole no. 81.

Pistol: ii. 1(43), 3(16) ; iii. 2(13), 6(21) ; iv. 1(17), 4(30) ; v. 1(23). Whole no. 163.

Nym: ii. 1(42), 3(5) ; iii. 2(6). Whole no. 53.

Bardolph: ii. 1(26), 3(6) ; iii. 2(2). Whole no. 34.

Boy: ii. 1(5), 3(9) ; iii. 2(34) ; iv. 4(32). Whole no. 80.

English Herald: iv. 8(1). Whole no. 1.

French King : ii. 4(42) ; iii. 5(28) ; v. 2(26). Whole no. 96.

Dauphin: ii. 4(38) ; iii. 5(11), 7(56) ; iv. 2(10), 5(6). Whole no. 121.

Constable: ii. 4(12) ; iii. 5(21), 7(60) ; iv. 2(29), 5(4). Whole no. 126.

Bourbon: iii. 5(9) ; iv. 5(9). Whole no. 18.

Orleans: iii. 7(41) ; iv. 2(3), 5(5). Whole no. 49.

Burgundy : v. 2(68). Whole no. 68.

Rambures: iii. 7(9) ; iv. 2(2). Whole no. 11.

Grandpré: iv. 2(18). Whole no. 18.

Governor of Harfleur: iii. 3(7). Whole no. 7.

Montjoy: iii. 6(25) ; iv. 3(13), 7(16). Whole no. 54.

1st Ambassador : i. 2(17). Whole no. 17.

French Soldier: iv. 4(20). Whole no. 20.

Messenger: ii. 4(2) ; iii. 7(3) ; iv. 2(1). Whole no. 6.

Queen Isabel : v. 2(24).   Whole no. 24.
Katherine : iii. 4(42) ; v. 2(31).   Whole no. 73.
Alice : iii. 4(24) ; v. 2(9).   Whole no. 33.
Hostess : ii. 1(17), 3(30).   Whole no. 47.
"*Chorus*": prol. (34) ; prol. ii. (42) ; prol. iii. (35) ; prol. iv. (53) ;
prol. v. (45) ; epil. (14)   Whole no. 223.
"*All*": v. 2(2).   Whole no. 2.

In the above enumeration, parts of lines are counted as whole lines,
making the total of the play greater than it is.   The actual number of
lines in each scene (Globe edition numbering) is as follows : prol. (34) ;
i. 1(98), 2(310) ; prol. ii. (42) ; ii. 1(133), 2(193), 3(66), 4(146) ; prol. iii.
(35) ; iii. 1(34), 2(153), 3(58), 4(66), 5(68), 6(181), 7(169) ; prol. iv. (53) ;
iv. 1(326), 2(63), 3(132), 4(82), 5(23), 6(38), 7(191), 8(131) ; prol. v. (45) ;
v. 1(94), 2(402) ; epil. (14).   Whole number in the play, 3380.

King Henry V. speaks more lines than any other character in Shakespeare.   Besides 1063 in this play, he has 616 in *1 Henry IV*. and 308
in *2 Henry IV*., making 1987 in all.   Falstaff comes next, having 719 in
1 Henry IV., 688 in *2 Henry IV*., and 488 in the *Merry Wives*, or 1895
in all.

INDEX OF WORDS EXPLAINED.

Fluellen. Stand away, Captain Gower; I will give treason his payment into plows, I warrant you (iv. 8. 11).